Parson & Jack Russell Terriers

DIANE MORGAN

Parson & Jack Russell Terriers

Project Team
Editor: Stephanie Fornino
Copy Editor: Joann Woy
Interior Design: Leah Lococo Ltd. and Stephanie Krautheim
Design Layout: Patricia Escabi

T.F.H. Publications
President/CEO: Glen S. Axelrod
Executive Vice President: Mark E. Johnson
Publisher: Christopher T. Reggio
Production Manager: Kathy Bontz

T.F.H. Publications, Inc.
One TFH Plaza
Third and Union Avenues
Neptune City, NJ 07753

Discovery Communications, Inc. Book Development Team
Maureen Smith, Executive Vice President & General
  Manager, Animal Planet
Carol LeBlanc, Vice President, Licensing
Elizabeth Bakacs, Vice President, Creative Services
Peggy Ang, Director, Animal Planet Marketing
Caitlin Erb, Licencing Specialist

Printed and bound in China

07 08 09 10 11 1 3 5 7 9 8 6 4 2

Library of Congress Cataloging-in-Publication Data
Morgan, Diane, 1947-
Parson & Jack Russell terriers / Diane Morgan.
p. cm. — (Animal planet pet care library)
Includes index.
ISBN-13: 978-0-7938-3774-8 (alk. paper) 1. Jack Russell terrier. I. Title. II. Title: Parson and Jack Russell terriers.
SF429.J27M67 2007
636.755—dc22
2006030266

This book has been published with the intent to provide accurate and authoritative information in regard to the subject matter within. While every precaution has been taken in preparation of this book, the author and publisher expressly disclaim responsibility for any errors, omissions, or adverse effects arising from the use or application of the information contained herein. The techniques and suggestions are used at the reader's discretion and are not to be considered a substitute for veterinary care. If you suspect a medical problem consult your veterinarian.

The Leader In Responsible Animal Care For Over 50 Years!™
www.tfh.com

Table of Contents

Chapter 1

Why I Adore My

Russell Terrier

Whether you call him a Jack or Parson Russell Terrier, this rough-and-tumble spitfire of a dog can charm almost anyone. Here is a dog who can run all day and play all night. He's handsome, clever, hardy, and happy. His multitudes of fans around the world praise him, and small wonder—this is one of the world's greatest and most complex dog breeds. He is not the world's easiest dog to own, but he's probably the most fun.

Do you understand where your Russell came from and how his past influences the dog he is today? To answer that, let's take a whirlwind tour of the Russell's history, because the past holds so many keys to the present.

History of the Parson and Jack Russell Terriers

The Russell Terrier began as an idea in the head of the Reverend John Russell (1795–1883), a clergyman living in the south of England. Although no indication exists that Parson Russell neglected his Sunday sermons, his great passion was foxhunting, a sport in which terriers, as well as traditional hounds, were included.

Parson Russell was looking for a "baying" terrier who would encourage the fox to run and so give more sport to the hunters on horseback. In the more northerly part of the country, which was extremely rocky, riding after hounds was not easy, and getting rid of pesky foxes was a chore rather than sport. In that part of the country, terriers were expected to dig down into the fox holes and kill the animal. Russell was more interested in a good ride, and he expected his terrier to

"bolt" the fox, which means to scare it and make it run, rather than kill it. Thus, Parson Russell developed a dog who was very similar to a foxhound, one who was long legged, lean, and harbored a love for the chase.

The Parson Russell Terrier Association of America

According to the Parson Russell Terrier Association of America (PRTAA), which was founded in 1985, things took a turn for the worse after the good reverend passed from this earth. Its members contend that as foxhunting became less and less common, people began to use their terriers to attack badgers by simply carrying them to the animal's lair and letting them go. This, they believed, encouraged a sort of aggressive behavior unlinked to the intelligence that the original breed needed to find the fox. And because the dog was needed to run down holes, he became short legged as well. The PRTAA maintains that this type of dog was imported to the United States as the "Jack Russell Terrier," and insists that the breed's founder would not have recognized this animal as something he

Did You Know?

Parson Russell was one of the founders of the English Kennel Club, in 1873. He also developed the Wire Fox Terrier.

bred. It is their opinion that the first breed standard, developed in 1904 by Arthur Heinemann, who later founded the Parson Jack Russell Terrier Club in 1914, reflects the Reverend Russell's original wishes by calling for a dog who is 14 inches (35.6 cm) high at the shoulder.

Today's PRTAA sets limits for the size of the Parson Russell Terrier at between 12 and 15 inches (30.5 cm and 38.1 cm). The PRTAA

Parson Russell wanted a baying terrier who would encourage the fox to run and give sport to the hunters on horseback.

specifically says that the "true" Parson Russell Terrier is a long-legged dog, similar in proportion to the foxhound, not a short-legged terrier as may be seen on occasion in the Jack Russell Terrier recognized by the Jack Russell Terrier Club of America (JRTCA).

On April 1, 2003, the American Kennel Club (AKC) began registering the breed as the "Parson Russell Terrier," although the breed was first registered in 1997 as the "Jack Russell Terrier." The name was changed to distinguish the PRTAA's idea of the Russell from the JRTCA's idea of the "Jack Russell." Today, the two clubs are completely different entities and not entirely on speaking terms.

At present, the PRTAA is recognized by the AKC as the parent club of the breed.

The Jack Russell Terrier Club of America

But there's history, and then there's history. And in this case, the JRTCA—the "other" (and larger) club—has a somewhat different take on events. It claims that the Russell has such a complex genetic inheritance that he is not a cookie-cutter style dog. Instead, the breed that this club calls the "Jack Russell Terrier" is known more for its work ethic than its looks, and members of the club believe that shorter-legged, smaller dogs are just as much a "Russell" as the longer-legged type. In fact, the JRTCA allows the terrier to be as small as 10 inches (25.4 cm).

Although the JRTCA hosts conformation shows, the emphasis in this club is on the dog's actual working ability. In fact, the JRTCA disputes the notion that these terriers did not go to ground after the fox—indeed, they believe that is the primary function of the terrier.

The JRTCA opposes any recognition of the Jack Russell by any kennel club or all-breed registry, because it believes that such recognition is detrimental to preserving the working characteristics and intelligence of the breed.

Differences Between the PRTAA and JRTCA

Although the differences between the PRTAA and JRTCA's standards are not critical to most pet owners, they are nevertheless revealing. Both breed clubs state that their major goal is to preserve the "original" working qualities of the breed. However, the JRTCA allows for a greater variation in size than does the PRTAA. And while the PRTAA/AKC standard is considerably more verbose than the one devised by the JRTCA, size is the main difference.

Currently, the situation regarding the breed is in flux. Whether the Jack Russell Terrier and the Parson Russell Terrier are one and the same breed or two different breeds depends on who you ask. (The British have their own version of the breed, with their own Kennel Club standard.) Because of the battling clubs, whose disagreement reaches into even what to call the breed, we'll refer to the dog as simply the "Russell," except where certain differences can absolutely be distinguished, to avoid as much confusion as possible.

The Kennel Club in England

The Kennel Club in England manages to get around all the controversy by suggesting that while the "ideal" height is 14 inches (35.6 cm) for males at the withers, smaller dogs are "quite acceptable" provided that they are sound. To this, the PRTAA merely says that "a 10-inch (25.4 cm) balanced terrier has none of the bone, substance, or stature necessary to satisfy breed function." It truly is an international family feud!

Physical Characteristics

Way back in 1871, Parson Russell himself described what he thought the ideal terrier should be and then went on to develop it. Russell was famous for his love of hunting and had a major hand in developing the Wire Fox Terrier as well as the Russell Terrier. Indeed, the Russell Terrier was originally designed to hunt foxes as part of his job, and much of both the PRTAA and JRTCA breed standards reflect that today.

General Appearance

The Russell is a strong, lively, intelligent,

predominately white dog. He is confident, alert, and tremendously charming.

Coat

Some Russells have a smooth coat, while others feature a rough or broken coat. The difference between these coats is a matter of some interpretation. Most people feel that a rough coat is the same as a broken coat, although some maintain that a slight difference exists between them, with the broken coat an intermediate between the rough and the smooth. It doesn't matter much, because rough, broken, and smooth are equally acceptable, as long as someone doesn't decide that the coat is woolly. In other words, the outer hair shouldn't have a soft or woolly feel to it.

The JRTCA finds a smooth, rough, or broken coat to be acceptable. The PRTAA recognizes a smooth or broken coat only.

Color

Today, both major Russell registries call for a mostly white dog. The JRTCA specifies that more than 51 percent of the dog's coat must be white, while the PRTAA settles for "predominantly white," which is about the same thing. Parson Russell himself confessed to have a great partiality to a white dog, possibly so that he could be easily distinguished from the red fox.

Today, both standards disallow a "brindled" dog, and there's a historical reason for that. Back in the old days, dogs who tried to kill a fox underground, rather than bringing it back up where the hunters could kill it themselves, were suspected of having "undesirable bull terrier blood," and bull terriers are often brindled. Therefore, the brindle color was outlawed. None of this makes complete sense in modern times, of course. But tradition is tradition.

Height and Weight

The PRTAA standard lists the ideal male Russell at 14 inches (35.6 cm) high at the highest point of the shoulder blade; females can get away with being 1 inch (2.5 cm) shorter. The animal's weight can range between 13 and 17 pounds (5.9 and 7.7 kg). The JRTCA permits dogs to measure between 10 and 15 inches (25.4 and 38.1 cm) at the shoulder but has no specific comment about weight.

Some people today use the word "shorty" to describe a Russell with shorter legs and a longer back. These physical characteristics are permitted under the JRTCA but not under PRTAA standards.

Spanning

Today, one of the most important physical measurements of the Russell is done by "spanning," a procedure meant to determine whether a dog is small enough to squeeze into an average-sized foxhole. Both Russell registries call for this procedure to be done by someone with average-size hands. To my mind, there's a problem here, since a considerable difference exists between an average-sized hand for a woman and a man.

To span your Russell, stand behind him, and simply place your hands around the dog's chest, right behind the elbows. If you can't touch your fingers together, you need bigger hands or a smaller dog. The JRTCA mentions that spanning should be a guide only, while the PRTAA says that it is very important.

Temperament and Personality

The Russell Terrier was bred first and foremost to be an independent, tough, go-to-ground hunter. Hunting dogs tend to bark, dig, and follow their noses. These are not "bad habits" but rather hard-wired natural behaviors. Unfortunately, many people use their heart and eyes rather than their common sense when acquiring a dog, and when the cuddly Russell begins to display these behaviors, he often ends up abandoned or in the pound. You must remember that your dog needs an outlet for his relentless energy, or he can become destructive,

Russells and Celebrities

Although celebrities such as Mariah Carey, Serena Williams, and Wynona Judd have owned Russells, certainly the most famous member of the breed in recent years is Eddie (real name "Moose") from the television show Frasier. Although Moose achieved a lot of publicity for the breed, it's important to know that a trained professional dog like this will probably bear scant resemblance to the one you own. In fact, too much publicity is a bad thing, and although Moose's charm attracted many naïve people to the breed, they soon found that living with a Russell is a challenge as well as a joy. (Sadly, Moose passed away in 2006.)

Your energetic Russell needs an outlet for his energy, or he can become destructive.

overprotective, and obsessive-compulsive.

In short, please be respectful of your dog's ancestry, because it is largely responsible for his temperament.

Aggression

All terriers can be aggressive with other dogs, cats, and smaller pets. With other dogs, the aggression is most common between animals of the same sex. However, because the Russell was bred to work in a pack, he can be taught to get along with other dogs if you socialize him early. But unless and until you are quite sure that your Russell gets along well with others, he should be an only pet or at least supervised continually in his interactions with other animals. I have known cases where, even though a Russell puppy was brought up with a kitten, instinct at last won out over family feeling, and the cat was eventually killed by his canine "friend." I am not saying that Russells and cats can't make good friends—they can. What I am saying is that you can't count on it.

Energy Level

Perhaps the key word in a Parson Russell's description has nothing to do with color, coat type, or even perfection of bodily form—it's "energetic." The Russell Terrier is a dynamo, so be prepared to accept and deal with this characteristic in your pet!

Speaking of lots of energy, digging is very natural for the Russell. For him, the world doesn't stop at ground level. Be prepared to make sacrifices in the beautiful lawn department, or else spend some time and effort making dig-safe areas.

Environment

Although Russells are meant to be country dogs, you can keep one in an apartment if you are dedicated enough to give him the exercise he needs—several times a day. However, because Russells can be barkers, thin walls and thin-skinned neighbors can be a problem. Although you might jump to the conclusion that a house in the suburbs is ideal, a lot depends on the tolerance of your neighbors and your own dog-keeping habits. Russells who are allowed to remain in the yard all day (or who are exiled to the outdoors) will tend to bark a great deal. So if you live in a house, make sure that your dog is in it when you leave.

Exercise Requirements

These dogs require a great deal of exercise, as do most hunting dogs. Small

does not equate to couch potato! One of the great things about Russell Terriers is that, unlike many other dogs, they will actually "self-exercise" in their yards. These creative dogs can think of plenty of things to keep themselves busy. Your Russell needs at least four half-hour periods of running play per day to keep him healthy, mentally stimulated, and happy. Remember, though, that even if your dog does enjoy running around by himself, he'll like it so much better if you're out there with him.

Intelligence

Because he is so intelligent, this terrier, above all others, must be more than a pet. Open your heart and home to this dynamic bundle of fur, but make sure that you give him ample opportunities do the things he loves by involving him in hunting, earth trials, agility, obedience, flyball, or other high-energy work. The Russell is much better at learning and even obeying commands than are most terriers, so he can excel in a variety of endeavors.

Trainability

To enjoy your terrier to the utmost, you must train and discipline him. These are highly intelligent and willful dogs, and they can often outsmart inexperienced owners. While they can be obedient, they are not as willing to please as Golden Retrievers—so don't be fooled into thinking that your Russell loves you so much that he'll follow you anywhere, on lead or off. He does love you, but his hunting heritage compels him to investigate every hole in the ground, break in the hedgerow, or opening in a fence. If he is not on the end of a leash, he must be securely fenced. (Check the fence weekly.) And when I say secure, I mean it. These dogs are equally great diggers and climbers. I once saw one scrabble over a 6-foot (1.8-m) chain link fence without turning a hair.

Protectiveness

Some Russells choose a family favorite and can become very protective of that person. This is something you must control. Terriers tend to be feisty as a rule, and while that can be a good trait, it can also be dangerous, because dogs don't always know burglars from friendly visitors. They can also be scrappy with each other, and many breeders strongly advise never to leave them alone with others of the same sex, because they could become aggressive. Respect your dog's terrier background, and remember that, while you should demand good manners, you have limited ability to alter your dog's genetic destiny.

The Russell is a challenging dog in many ways, but he's also a special one. If you enjoy a smart, independent thinker with an unlimited capacity for

FAMILY-FRIENDLY TIP

Puppies and Kids: A Russell Can Tussle!

Russell Terriers are extremely tough, playful dogs who make excellent companions for children. However, they will not suffer abuse at the hand of any child, and the independent Russell will stand up for himself fiercely if necessary.

Always supervise interactions between children and dogs. Children must be taught to leave a puppy alone while he is eating or sleeping, never to chase or yell at a puppy, and to pet a puppy quietly. Dogs cannot always be expected to know the difference between exuberance and meanness, and neither can a young child. In addition, children do not instinctively understand puppy teething behavior and also are frequently scratched by those puppy nails. Remember, it's up to you as the parent to teach children how to interact with puppies kindly and safely.

play and fun, if you want a dog whose undivided loyalty will do you proud, and if you have the patience and sense of humor to appreciate a "terrier treasure," you couldn't have chosen a better breed.

Chapter 2

The Stuff of

Everyday Life

The Russell Terrier is a pretty self-sufficient dog, but even the most independent of creatures needs a few accoutrements to fit snugly into his new human family. And until your dog is issued his own credit card, it's up to you to buy or make the things that keep him safe and happy.

Baby Gates

You probably don't want your precious puppy wandering all around the house unsupervised, so you must block off certain rooms and the stairway. Choose a baby gate that's approved by consumer organizations; you can get some made especially for dogs. If your dog is a major chewer, though, don't get a wooden gate.

Bed

Your Russell needs his own bed. Choose a sturdy one that is resistant to chewing (not wicker, which can break off into sharp, unpleasant fragments that can lodge in or pierce your puppy's esophagus, tummy, or intestines). The bedding can be made of any soft, washable material; the "sheepskin" kind is often favored. However, plain old towels or an unwashed tee-shirt that carries your scent will work too.

There's even an allergen-resistant bed, made from "breathable" Cordura nylon, a

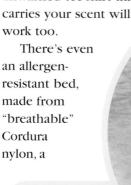

A plain soft buckle collar is all you really need for the Russell Terrier.

washable fabric tougher than cotton or fleece, which traps dust and other allergy-causing particles.

Cleaning Supplies

Non-ammonia–based cleaners and carpet deodorizers are good to have on hand. And don't forget the paper towels—lots of them.

Collar

A plain soft buckle collar is really all you need. For highly energetic dogs like Russells, who can get caught in fences, one obvious choice is the break-away collar. This has a safety buckle that opens the collar but can still be used securely with a leash.

Make sure that your Russell's collar fits correctly. You'll know it fits properly if you can insert two fingers between the collar and your dog's neck.

To add safety to your standard collar, consider ordering a MicroID collar that allows owners to place a flash card memory device on the collar. This card stores all kinds of information about the pet and is embedded in the collar, so it can't tear free. It also includes a toll-free number in case the finder has no access to a USB jack.

Choke Chains

A big debate surrounds the use of choke-chain collars, because incorrect usage can result in neck injury, especially for a puppy. You will achieve better, longer-lasting results using positive reinforcement and plain old buckle collars.

Halter

Although several versions of the halter exist, one basic design consists of one strap that encircles your dog's nose and another that goes around his neck and behind his ears. Instead of pulling on the neck, the halter puts gentle pressure on the muzzle, which has the simultaneous effects of calming the animal and controlling him.

The head halter is very popular with some people, but most dogs really don't like it, and almost all will resist it, at least at first. It is, however, particularly useful for controlling aggressive or dominant dogs, including those who like to squabble with others. It may even help control dogs who have major issues, like food aggression and biting. It is also very handy for those dogs who like to pull.

The trickiest thing about the head halter is getting it to fit properly. If it doesn't, it will be both uncomfortable

FAMILY-FRIENDLY TIP

Should Your Child Care for the Dog?

Although your Russell may turn out to be your child's best friend, he is your responsibility. Even well-intentioned children can forget to feed, walk, or water a dog. Be resigned to taking care of the dog yourself or carefully overseeing the child while she fulfills her promise to care for him.

and ineffective. The neck strap should be as high up on the neck as possible and just tight enough so that you can get one finger between it and the dog's neck.

Harnesses

Some people prefer harnesses, especially for puppies. They are very safe but provide less control than do other methods. One exception is a front-loop harness; this device has a loop low on the front instead of along the back that makes walking even a difficult dog a breeze. Harnesses are also good for dogs with spinal problems or for sensitive dogs who don't like collars and head halters.

Crate

Next to eating, sleeping is a high priority for most dogs, and a crate is a safe, comfortable place for that activity. Although crates may look like a cage, a properly trained Russell has no such prejudice. He thinks of the crate as a safe haven—a den of his own. In addition, a crate is a great housetraining tool. A crate is not a place of banishment or a babysitter, though, and dogs should not be locked in their crates for more than two hours at a time, except for at night when they should be sleeping. This doesn't mean that your dog has to sleep in a crate, of course. Mine never do. But he should be taught to accept a comfortable crate when asked. This is important for traveling or when the dog is sick and must have his activity restricted. Your dog's crate or bed should be off-limits to kids.

Whatever crate you and your dog choose, be sure to provide a soft, cushy, washable mat for your dog's sleeping comfort. (When you are housetraining, however, you may want to omit the mat, because dogs are often driven to urinate on soft, absorbable surfaces.)

Be sure to buy the right size cage, one with sufficient floor space for the puppy to lie down. You can actually get a much larger crate, of course, but for housetraining purposes, choose a model that comes with divider panels as an accessory. These will allow you to adjust the area of the crate. In housetraining, as

The crate is a safe, comfortable place for your Russell to sleep and eat.

you will see, you want to discourage the puppy from using his crate as a bathroom, so keep the area small.

Crates come in three basic styles: wire mesh, sturdy fiberglass or plastic, and fold-up nylon mesh. Each has its distinct advantages, and many dog owners eventually end up with one of each. Your Russell's crate should be not only high enough for him to stand up in (an easy requirement) but big enough for him to turn around in easily (harder to meet) and to stretch out in completely.

Wire

The wire crate offers the best ventilation and vision. Once inside, your dog can look around and see what's happening. This type of crate is wonderful in the summer, when your dog can take advantage of the breezes blowing through. On the other hand, a wire crate offers no protection from the sun (unless you drape it with towel) or cold wind.

Fiberglass or Plastic

The fiberglass or plastic crate is very tough and good for traveling and sleeping. It provides the most den-like atmosphere, and many dogs feel especially secure.

Fold-Up Nylon Mesh

The new fold-up nylon mesh crates are indispensable for traveling and quick setup. They can go anywhere! Their main disadvantage is that a dog not used to crates can tear it with his claws.

Doggy Door

The doggy door is the housetrainer's dream and the working owner's friend. It allows your easily bored and independent terrier access to the thrilling world of your fenced backyard. Russells are so smart that they get the hang of it very quickly. You can always purchase one of the simple ones with a clear, flexible plastic panel, or you can spend your hard-earned cash on an ultra high-tech, pet-activated model with an automatic safety retract system, dual-range controls, and an automatic deadbolt lock. A lot depends on what kind of neighborhood you live in.

Exercise Pen

An exercise pen (x-pen) is your Russell's very own recreation area. It's an excellent way for him to get safe exercise while you're not watching him, and it even helps with introductions, because the open steel wire construction will allow him to view, but not immediately

Setting Up a Schedule

If you think you're too busy to set up a schedule, think again. Busy families are in the most need for imposing order in their lives, and that's where a schedule comes in really handy. When both owner and dog know when it's time for feeding, playtime, and bathroom business, an atmosphere of calm prevails. Dogs who never know when or if they are going to be fed or walked tend to be anxious and hyperactive. A regular schedule helps your dog feel secure and aids in housetraining, thus contributing to his overall development.

interact with, anything in the vicinity—like another dog, the family cat, or your new baby. When you are too busy to pay strict attention to your Russell's wanderings, the x-pen will keep him in a spot where you know he is not getting into any major trouble. All sizes and heights are available.

Food and Water Bowls

Because your Russell will need a supply of cool, clean water at all times, as well as food, he needs his own set of dishes. I prefer to use stainless steel to feed my own dogs, because these bowls are inexpensive, hardy, and easy to clean. Ceramic dishes are prettier, though, and are also suitable. Both come in weighted varieties that resist being tipped over by a playful puppy.

I don't recommend plastic bowls for a few reasons. First, Russells can and will chew through cheap plastic, and second, plastic can develop cracks and gaps that harbor dangerous bacteria. Also, dogs who eat out of plastic bowls can develop a nasty dermatitis on the skin caused by an allergy to plastic.

Whatever style you choose, you should wash the bowls frequently in hot soapy water, just as you would your own crockery.

Licensing

Most localities require you to get a license for your dog. Don't ignore this requirement. For one thing, the money you spend on the license often goes to help the local SPCA. A license is also another form of identification, and you can't have too much of that! For another, it's the law. In New York, for example, all dogs over the age of 6 months must be licensed. Other states and localities have different requirements, so check with your local government to see what laws apply. Some places also require additional fees for people owning more than a certain number of dogs.

Grooming Supplies

To keep your Russell looking sharp, you'll need the following:
- brushes and combs
- shampoo
- cotton balls
- nail clippers or a grinder
- canine toothbrush and toothpaste

A grooming table may also come in handy, although it's not a necessity.

Identification

Every year, 8 to 10 million pets are lost; only a fraction ever return to their homes. You can increase the odds by properly identifying your dog. You can do this with a collar and dog tag, a tattoo, or a microchip.

Collar and Tag

The collar and tag are the most traditional and visible methods of identification. Simply put a current telephone number (yours and your vet's) on the tag. You don't need to put your name or the dog's name on it. It's also a good idea to use a riveted nameplate or write your phone number directly on the collar. Your dog should wear this ID even if he has another form of identification.

Tattoo

A tattoo on the inside of your dog's thigh or on the abdomen is another possibility. The tattoo is usually a number linking the dog to a registry. It is important to keep your information current with the registry, however, or the information will be useless.

Microchip

A microchip implant the size of a grain of rice can be inserted between a dog's shoulder blades, and a scanner wand is used to read it. One problem is that the chips can sometimes migrate under the skin, making finding them more difficult. The advantages of the chip far outweigh

this disadvantage, though. Unlike most dog tags or tattoos, the chip won't become illegible over time, which means that your pet has a permanent method of identification. At one time, different chips made by different companies needed different scanners, but this problem has been essentially solved so that just about any scanner can read any chip.

Leash

You should have a regular 4- to 6-foot (1.2- to 1.8-m) leash made of leather, waxed cotton, or nylon. Chain leashes are noisy, heavy, and unnecessary. They give no warning when they are about to break, and they can develop sharp

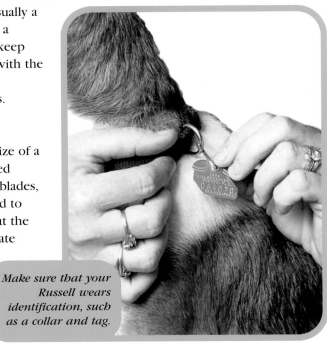

Make sure that your Russell wears identification, such as a collar and tag.

edges. Good leather leashes are durable and comfortable, especially as they age. However, leather leashes are slow to dry out once they get wet. They are also attractive to a dog's taste buds, so never let your terrier take the leash in his mouth. Once he gets a taste for it, you're doomed. (Some owners spray their leather leashes with a bitter apple spray or a similar aversive product to discourage chewing, but it doesn't always work.) Beware of cheap leather leashes, which can be rough on your hands.

Pooper Scooper

Of course, you will want to pick up your dog's mess. For this unpleasant but necessary task, you can purchase a sophisticated, back-saving, long-handled "pooper scooper," or you can just get a plastic bag and pick it up. So much depends on your sensibilities. The dog won't care either way, and neither will your neighbors, as long as the waste is removed.

Dog Walkers

If you can't get home during the day to walk or otherwise exercise your dog, consider hiring a dog walker. A dog walker can be a bonded professional or a neighborhood kid whom you know and trust. It doesn't matter whom you choose, as long as your Russell gets that scheduled exercise. You'll both be happier!

Adaptability of Older Russells

Most Russells adapt quickly to their new homes as long as they have the loving support of their new family. It is a myth that older dogs don't bond easily to new people. In fact, they often bond even more quickly than does a puppy. To make sure this happens, be prepared to give the dog sufficient attention. If you do, he will soon reciprocate.

Toys

Dogs love toys. They not only like to chase them, chew placidly on them, and cuddle up next to them, but they also (especially terriers) like to rip them to pieces. In fact, there's no sense in telling your dog to "play nicely." He's a terrier, and terriers are infamous chewers.

Because your dog needs to chew, consider creating inexpensive toys that won't break your bank account. For a fun and inexpensive toy, take a plastic water bottle and remove the label. Throw away the top. Voila! A new fetch toy! These containers are

If your Russell enjoys tugging games, a rope toy is a good choice.

too light to hurt your dog. Your Russell will crunch it all up, of course, and that's when you can throw it away and drag out another one. This is recycling at its finest.

If you must buy a toy, buy one that gives those tough terrier jaws some exercise. Hard rubber toys are great favorites, especially if you sneak a little cheese, peanut butter, or kibble inside them. Dogs enjoy toys with squeakers, but if you have an aggressive chewer, there's a chance that he might remove and swallow it.

If your Russell enjoys tugging games, a rope toy is a natural, and these kinds of toys have the added benefit of being good for the teeth. If he's a cuddler and not too destructive, a soft cloth toy will be a comfort to him.

Don't give in to your natural wish to buy or make your dog every toy on the planet. Instead, keep some in the cupboard or on top of the refrigerator, and rotate them. Because Russells are like children and become bored easily, this will keep him interested in his toys.

Whatever toys you choose, make sure that they are washable and have no detachable bits that your dog can swallow.

Altogether, your Russell's requirements are quite simple. He doesn't need artwork, video games, or a library full of rare books. All he needs are some basic supplies to keep him happy and safe. Sometimes a simple life is the most fulfilling!

Chapter 3

Good Eating

No one expects you to cook your dog's food in a chemical laboratory and measure every single ingredient. We don't feed ourselves that way. It's neither possible nor necessary. But you must pay attention to your dog's diet, because you are responsible for what he eats.

Your dog depends on you to feed him what he needs, so do the research to provide him with the best diet that you possibly can.

Necessary Nutrients

Eating is a fun way to gather in important nutrients, such as carbohydrates, fats, minerals, proteins, vitamins, and water. These nutrients that your dog needs work synergistically. For example, a specific metabolic reaction may take ten steps, each requiring a different nutrient. If even one of these nutrients is missing or deficient, it's as if all ten were missing. That's why it's so important to feed a nutritious, balanced diet.

Commercial Food

Today, about 95 percent of American dog owners feed their dogs primarily or solely a commercial diet, usually dry kibble. Americans spend billions of dollars every year on pet food (more than on baby food!). In fact, we have thousands of different pet foods from which to choose. Although most of these products contain the minimum amounts of nutrients to be considered "nutritionally complete," none of them is really an ideal food for your dog. Their greatest advantage is that they are convenient.

Food Labels

Dog food labels are regulated by not one but several branches of the US government, including the Food and Drug Administration and the Department of Agriculture. (In some ways, the labels are more strictly regulated than what goes inside the can or bag.)

Pet food labels have two main parts: the information panel and the principal display panel. The principal display panel is used to make the product look attractive to the customer—you. It must include a product name that identifies the product as a pet food; it usually also includes a manufacturer's name or a brand name as well. The weight of the product is also included.

The information panel contains a list of ingredients, the guaranteed analysis, feeding instructions, and nutritional adequacy claim. Look for a statement on the bag that says that the product successfully passed feeding trials of the Association of American Feed Control Officials (AAFCO). This ensures that the food has at least the minimum amount of nutritional value that your dog needs.

The best commercial foods:
• contain no meat by-products

- contain no sweeteners, artificial flavors, colors, or preservatives
- do not contain an excess amount of carbohydrates
- are preserved naturally with vitamin E (tocopherols) or vitamin C
- contain the specific name of a meat (beef, chicken, turkey) as the first ingredient

Whatever brand of food you choose, go for quality. The difference between the best and worst commercial foods is just a little money per bag, but the difference in nutrition can add healthy years to your dog's life.

Table Manners

Both dogs and owners should have good table manners. Your part of promoting good pet etiquette requires that you feed your dog on time, leave him alone while he eats, and wash his dishes afterward. His job is to eat his dinner. I like to feed my dogs at the same time I eat—the dogs got the idea very quickly that we each have our own food and our own place to sit. If you want to give your dog a healthy treat from your plate, do it after you eat, and put the food in his dish. Do not allow him to beg from the table.

Dry Food (Kibble)

Kibble is a convenient, nutritionally adequate food for dogs. In comparison with other food choices, dry food is the least expensive, largely because of its high grain content. Dry food also tends to be low in fat, which is good if your dog is overweight or inactive.

Don't be seduced by fancy colors and shapes. Shape doesn't matter, and the colors come from vegetable dye, not food nutrients. Some people like to feed their dogs a basic diet of kibble with different added foods every day, such as green beans, carrots, gravy, or canned meat. This plan gives your dog adequate nutrition and variety.

Canned Food

Although some canned dog food smells unpleasant to us, most dogs prefer the aroma and flavor. Canned food is much more expensive than kibble and is usually about 75 percent water. Canned foods can also be high in fat. These foods can be useful for mixing with dry food, however, because most dogs find canned foods to be highly palatable. Dogs who have urinary tract infections often do better on canned dog foods than on kibble, mostly because of the increased water intake provided by canned foods.

Semi-Moist Food

Semi-moist food is about 25 percent

water and can be just as high in sugar, in the form of corn syrup, beet pulp, sucrose, and caramel. Your dog does not need this stuff, which promotes obesity and tooth decay. The shelf life of these products is also lower than either canned or dry food.

Kibble is a convenient, nutritionally adequate food for dogs.

Noncommercial Food

Although you wouldn't believe it to hear some dog food commercials, you can actually create a perfectly healthy diet for your dog at home, just as you can for your own family.

Home-Cooked Diet

If you are dedicated to providing the perfect diet for your dog, the best plan is a home-prepared, well-researched diet. The advantages of a homemade diet are obvious: You can tailor it to your own dog's particular needs, and you'll be using quality ingredients that don't include artificial preservatives and by-products. Although people often claim that home-prepared diets are more expensive than commercial ones,

you can largely offset this factor by including healthy leftovers from your own meals.

Preparing a diet at home does require some training. The main dangers from such diets are a calcium/phosphorus imbalance and inadequate levels of calcium, copper, iodine, and certain vitamins, especially fat-soluble and some B vitamins, so you'll need to do your research. Many excellent books have published recipes for healthy

Storing Food Safely

If you use a commercial food, check the manufacturing date. Do not buy in bulk—it may save you some money, but it's dangerous for your dog. Smaller bags get used more quickly and stay fresher longer. Store the food in a dry, cool place away from sunlight and temperature fluctuations. Most food should be kept in its original packaging or in a special airtight container. One of the best rules of thumb is that if the food smells bad, throw it out.

Make sure that your Russell has a constant supply of cool, fresh water.

homemade diets that you can adapt for your own purposes.

In short, nothing is better for your dog than a properly prepared home-cooked diet.

Raw Diet

Over the past several years, many people have begun feeding their dogs raw foods in the belief that such foods are more natural and healthier than cooked foods. Certainly, a raw diet is one that wolves have evolved on for many millions of years, but then again, wolves are not eating meat that may have been contaminated in slaughterhouses, either. And it may certainly be true that high-quality raw meat is better than what you may normally get in commercial foods.

However, no evidence whatsoever suggests that a raw-meat diet is healthier for your dog than the same meat cooked. Raw meat is especially dangerous for dogs with compromised immune systems, and it can cause fatal *Salmonella* infections.

If you are considering a raw diet, talk to your veterinarian.

Bones

Dogs adore bones, but they can be harmful because they can easily splinter, damaging your dog's throat and digestive system in the process. This applies to both cooked and raw bones. The "sterilized bones" that you can buy in the store are very dangerous in this regard—they are unnaturally hard and can cause broken teeth.

The most dangerous consequence of bone consumption is a perforated intestine, which allows toxins to escape into the dog's system.

Treats

At first glance, treats seem to have no downside—people enjoy giving them, and dogs enjoy getting them. Still, not all treats are created equal. Cow hoofs, for example, are quite dangerous. In fact, they are the number-one cause of tooth breakage in dogs. Rawhide is another example of a potentially dangerous treat. Dogs chew it up like gum and then swallow it, and it can stick in a dog's throat. Even if he gets it down, rawhide is not good for the digestive system. To make matters worse, some rawhide treats are basted with flavors that disagree with the canine digestive system, causing diarrhea. If you notice this, switch to plain, unbleached rawhide treats, or omit them altogether.

Dogs have strong opinions when it comes to the perfect treat flavor, and despite the recent plethora of melon, vanilla, and peanut butter delights, most dogs like liver treats.

Feeding for Every Life Stage

Mammals are programmed to be hungry all the time, but in most cases, dogs should be fed on a schedule rather than free fed (a method that involves setting the food dish down all day so that the dog can eat at his leisure). It's difficult to monitor how much a free-fed dog is actually consuming, and if you own more than one dog, you won't know who's getting the food. In addition, studies have shown that free feeding is very strongly linked with obesity.

If you want a fit dog, feed him a proper amount at scheduled times— don't let him decide for himself. Dogs don't make very good decisions about these things. In fact, the genetic heritage of dogs encourages them to gorge when food is available, and even though your Russell hasn't been out hunting caribou in a while, his genes don't know that. Where food is concerned, he thinks he's still a wolf. The bottom line? Don't free feed your dog.

FAMILY-FRIENDLY TIP

Children and Feeding the Family Dog

If your child would like to be involved in your dog's dinnertime, show her how. Even a young child can be trained to notice when the water bowl is empty. Older children can learn to pour and serve dinner. How much your child participates in the project depends on her level of maturity.

In most cases, dogs should be fed on a schedule rather than free fed.

Feeding a Puppy

Young puppies (two to four months) must eat four times a day, usually a high-quality kibble softened with some warm water. You can add some yogurt, canola or safflower oil, or cottage cheese for palatability. From four to six months, you may reduce the number of meals to three, and reduce to two meals a day at six months of age.

Feeding an Adult

When a terrier reaches the age of one year, some people start feeding only once a day. However, twice-daily feedings seem to better suit most dogs.

Feeding a Senior

As your Russell ages, he will become less active and consequently need fewer calories. If you are feeding a high-quality dog food, you can safely reduce the amount he eats. Lesser quality dog foods, however, contain just enough vitamins and minerals to keep your dog going at the amount indicated, so you will have to supplement with vitamins and minerals. (Be sure to consult your veterinarian.) Senior dogs often have special dietary needs; however, most commercial foods designed for seniors take these into account.

Obesity

Sixty percent of all adult dogs in the United States are overweight, a fact that affects their health, enjoyment of life, and ability to participate in normal dog activities. Obesity also increases the likelihood of developing heart, liver, and kidney disease, as well as diabetes and arthritis. Studies show that the only "supplement" to actually help your pet live longer is to cut down on his caloric intake.

Obesity is defined as being 10 to 25 percent above the ideal weight for your dog. An adult Russell should weigh between 13 and 17 pounds (5.9 and 7.7 kg). To determine whether your Russell is obese, look at him from above; he should resemble an hourglass. Too much bulge in the waist indicates that your dog should be put on a diet. If you touch with your thumbs along your dog's spine, you should be able feel each rib. If you must put pressure on the rib cage to feel the ribs, your dog is overweight. (If you can actually see your dog's ribs, he's too thin.) When viewed from the side, you should see a "tucked-up" waist.

If you use dog treats as a training aid and your Russell is obese, cut back on the amount of regular food you give your dog, and use treats that have some nutritional value. No matter how much fun it is to feed your dog, and no matter how much he enjoys eating,

When given the right food in the right amounts, your Russell will thrive.

remember: Obesity will shorten his life. Replace high-caloric treats with nutritious, crispy carrots, and add fresh vegetables like broccoli to your dog's dinner. Just as with humans, the key is a low-fat, high-fiber diet. Unless you're an expert on home-prepared foods, use a high-quality weight-loss commercial brand. The manufacturer has done the hard part by providing the correct amounts of vitamins and minerals. Remember to change from one brand of food to another gradually over a period of a week or two, especially if your dog is a picky eater or has a sensitive stomach.

Although most cases of obesity are caused by the fatal combination of overfeeding and underexercising, in a few instances, a medical condition such as hypothyroidism or insulin imbalance could be at fault. It's important not to put your dog on a weight-loss program until you check with your veterinarian to make sure that no underlying medical problem exists.

Once you find that you and your Russell are in the clear, provide more brisk, aerobic exercise for him. A human-paced walk of a mile or two (1.6 or 3.2 km) does almost nothing to burn calories for your dog. He needs to

SENIOR DOG TIP

Feeding the Senior Dog

Older dogs have less muscle mass than they used to, and so they need fewer calories to maintain their bodies. At the same time, they need better nutrition as they age, because their bodies are less efficient at metabolizing food. So that's the prescription for older dogs— feed lower calorie but higher quality foods.

run, and if no fenced dog park or safe area is available near you, you'll have to help him out by actively playing with him. Getting him an energetic doggy companion will help, too. Begin any exercise program gradually, and use common sense.

When given the right food in the right amount, you will see your Russell blossom into the most healthy and joyful of pets.

Good Eating

Chapter **4**

Looking Good

Grooming your dog not only improves his appearance and adds to his comfort but also makes him a healthier dog. While you are grooming your Russell, you are bound to notice problems that crop up, and so you can tend to them earlier.

If you begin grooming your Russell when he is very young, you will have very little trouble later on. And if you set aside only five minutes a day for a quick brushing, you'll find that your terrier is almost maintenance free!

Grooming Supplies

Before you begin grooming your Russell, it's a good idea to have the supplies you need on hand. They include:

- bristle brush
- canine shampoo (formulated for rough and broken coats)
- canine toothbrush and toothpaste
- ear cleaner
- nail clippers
- plastic apron
- scissors (for rough and broken coats)
- towels
- wide-toothed metal combs

If you plan to strip your Russell's rough or broken coat, you'll also need two stripping blades. As for your grooming tools, don't be cheap. Better quality tools cost more, but they work better and last longer. Trying to save a little money now and ending up spending a lot more later is false economy.

Brushing

A thorough brushing is the foundation of good coat care. Russells come in two basic coat types: smooth and rough (or broken). The smooth version has a straight, hard "jacket" or outer coat, with a softer, dense undercoat. The same is true, of course, for the rough (or broken) coat, but in this case, the outer coat is rough, not smooth. Both types, but especially the smooth, are

Use good-quality grooming tools, because they work well and last a long time.

easy to care for. (The rough and broken coats are a little harder to care for than the smooth coat, but shed less.)

Always brush your dog before bathing him, not after. If you bathe a dog who has mats in his coats, the bathing process will turn the mats into hard little balls that you'll have to cut out.

How to Brush the Smooth Coat

The tools you need to groom the smooth coat are simple: a firm, natural-bristle brush, metal combs, and scissors. The scissors are to remove stray hairs only, not to sculpt the body to give it an unnatural appearance.

Always be methodical in your grooming. Start at the head and work downward. (If you have a dog who really objects to the process, though, you may get better results by starting at the hindquarters. Dogs usually find that more bearable, and you can slowly move toward the head.) Use light, downward strokes, and check for mats as you brush. Leave the sensitive areas until last. While you are brushing, you might want to put one hand on the dog to comfort him and keep him stable.

You may wish to finish with a light mist of conditioning gloss, but it is certainly not necessary.

The Expert Knows

Grooming as a Health Check

Grooming your dog regularly gives you a chance to examine him carefully for lumps, cuts, sores, bad breath, goopy eyes, inflamed ears, split nails, and other warnings of a potential health problem.

How to Brush the Rough or Broken Coat

To brush the rough or broken coat, a regular slicker brush works to get rid of excess dirt and hair. However, you also need special equipment for stripping these types of coats, including a wide-toothed comb, wire brush, and two short, serrated knives (one with a dull blade and one with a sharp blade). Thinning shears may also come in handy.

Most of the same rules apply to a rough or broken coat as to a smooth, but you have to do a few more things. For the rough or broken coat, grooming accomplishes more than promoting good health and comfort. Doing it the right way will help your Russell get his coat into top-notch rain-proofing condition by making it "hard."

Looking Good

The Grooming Table

A grooming table is very helpful, although it's not an absolute necessity. The traditional grooming table is foldable and easily transportable. It usually stands about 30 inches (76.2 cm) high and has ribbed rubber matting. Whatever surface your dog stands on should be nonslip. Most grooming tables have a grooming post with a noose for holding your dog still while you groom. A dog should stand while being groomed.

The rough or broken coat requires a special kind of handling. Hair remains in the shaft long after it has ceased to grow, and although it will get pushed out eventually, the coat tends to look unkempt unless it is properly "plucked" or "stripped." People who show the rough- or broken-coated Russell must strip the coat, a job most easily done by a professional. (Ideally, professional stripping is done twice a year.) However you can learn to do it yourself. This will not bother the dog if you go slowly. Doing this carefully not

only removes the dead hair but ensures an even, new growth of coarse hair, which is what you want in this type of coat. If you don't pluck it, the new hair will grow in too fine, and the dog won't have the proper coat. If you don't want to go through all this, you can use some electric clippers to keep the coat trim. It will lack the hardness and the look of a perfect show coat, but it will suffice if your dog is not going to be shown.

To brush the coat, start with a densely packed wire slicker brush. (You can alternatively use a "dresser" comb and blade available at your local pet supply shop.) The general rule is to brush or comb the hair away from the direction of hair growth and then pull out the dead hair in the direction of the growth. Always do just small sections at a time. To make it easier on you and the dog, coat your fingers with cornstarch or use rubber thimbles on your fingers to give you a good grasp of the dead hair.

To strip your Russell's coat, follow the steps listed below:

1. First, pull out facial hair in the direction of growth. Make sure both sides are even. You may want to leave some whiskers around the face to give it some definition and preserve your dog's character.
2. Then, rake your fingers down the back of the neck, pull the skin taut, and pluck a few hairs at a time, moving slowly to the front. (The

hair around the cowlick may be particularly long or troublesome.) When you are done, you way wish to take the sharper knife and very gently comb in the direction of the hair growth.

3. Next, move to the chest area, following the same procedure.

4. Then, move to the legs. You may notice that the "bumps" on the knees are just clumps of hair that come away as you groom your dog. Use the scissors to trim the hair on the toes.

5. Move to the back, always keeping the skin taut and plucking dead hair in the direction of its growth. Don't forget the anal area— plucking here helps to keep the area clean. Use the dull knife to get rid of the excess hair here. You can keep the skin taut by pulling up gently on the tail. Male dogs may also have extra hair around the sheath of the penis that should be scissored away.

6. Finish up with the tail itself, following the same basic plucking procedure. Make sure to clip the extra hairs at the end of the tail to give it a neater appearance. You may then go over the entire dog with the dull stripping knife.

After you're finished, bathe your dog in cool water to close his pores. In a few days, check everything over to make sure that you haven't missed any hairs. Because stripping is done almost only by people who show their dogs, the general rule on how often to strip is six to eight weeks before a show.

Bathing

Generally, your terrier can be bathed twice a month. If you are showing a rough- or broken-coated Russell, though, avoid giving him a wet bath less than a week before the show. Shampoo, even the kind designed for terriers, can oversoften the coat. Use a dry shampoo before the show if you must.

For bathing, you'll need:
- absorbent towels
- plastic apron
- doggy shampoo (some kinds are especially designed for rough- or broken-coated dogs)

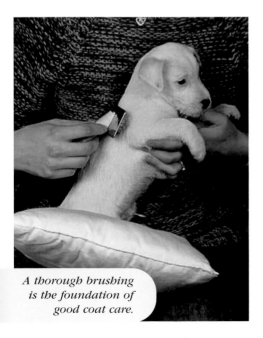

A thorough brushing is the foundation of good coat care.

- skidproof mat for the bathtub
- sponge or washcloth
- tether that attaches by suction cup to the wall (if your dog is hard to handle in the bathtub)

How to Bathe Your Russell

To bathe your Russell, turn the warm to warm—not as hot as you would use for yourself. (Dogs have thinner skins and so are more sensitive to water temperature.) Put a screen in the drain to catch the hair. Then, soak your dog completely. The rough- or broken-coated variety's coat is somewhat water resistant, so this may take some doing. Put your thumb over his ears so that water doesn't inadvertently run in them. Then, apply a shampoo-soaked sponge and work up a good lather in the direction of hair growth. Use plenty of soap, and be very careful to avoid the eyes.

When your dog is thoroughly soaped up, rinse him carefully (shampoo left in the coat causes itchy skin), then rub him briskly using at least two warmed towels. The more water you get off now, the faster he will dry. You can also use a hair dryer. If you are using a dryer designed for humans, use the coolest setting. A drying temperature warmer

than room temperature can give your dog's rough or broken coat a case of the frizzies, the exact opposite of the kind of coat you want. If you have a broken- or rough-coated dog, use a soft brush and cloth to rub the coat flat to the body, and let it dry slowly.

Don't use an oil-based product on these coats, because it will damage their desirable harsh texture.

Dental Care

Periodontal disease has reached epidemic proportions in the family dog. More than 80 percent of all dogs have it by three years of age! To prevent this disease, brush your Russell's teeth every day with specially

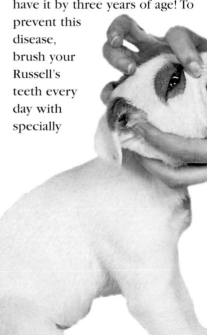

Brushing and inspecting your Russell's teeth daily will help prevent periodontal disease.

formulated canine toothpaste to prevent plaque and tartar buildup, which causes tooth loss.

How to Care for Your Russell's Teeth

If your puppy or older dog is not used to having his teeth brushed, start by just putting some of the toothpaste on your fingertip so that your dog can see how good the stuff is. Within a short period, you will be able to massage the gums and teeth, and from there it's only a small step to real brushing. When your Russell is ready to accept brushing, use a circular motion with the toothbrush. However, it's a lot easier just to brush back and forth, and this motion probably works as well, too.

Ear Care

Your dog needs his ears to hear with. If his ears are clean and healthy, he can do this admirably, but if they are dirty, crammed with earwax, or infected, he will not only be unable to hear very well, he'll be in serious discomfort.

How to Care for Your Russell's Ears

Clean your Russell's ears with a cotton ball or soft cloth soaked in ear cleaner once a week. Avoid the urge to use a cotton swab—it's easy to go too far into the ear canal and damage it. A cotton ball is a better choice. Choose a

Getting Rid of Awful Things

It's inevitable. Dogs get things stuck, tangled, and embedded in their hair—especially the active Russell—and it's up to you to fix the problem. Here's how:

- **Gum:** Cut out carefully with scissors.
- **Sap:** Try using an emulsifying dish soap. If that doesn't work, use scissors.
- **Skunk smell:** Use a commercial de-skunker. Tomato juice does not work.
- **Tar:** Apply petroleum jelly followed by bathing. Do not use turpentine or kerosene.

commercial, non-alcohol-based ear wash or a good herbal product with mullein to bring wax and dirt to the surface.

To clean your Russell's ears, just massage them gently. Don't insert anything deeply into the ear, because you could damage the delicate tissues. (A dog's ear is L-shaped, so you can't get to the bottom of it anyway.)

If your dog pulls away or resists having you examine an ear, suspect trouble. Dark, gritty material in the ears may signal ear mites. You can't see mites without magnification, but an infected dog may scratch the hair off the back of his ears for relief. You can buy a commercial cleaner to get rid of

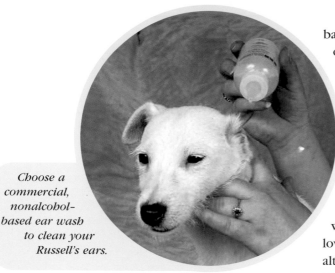

them. Red, smelly, or inflamed ears indicate a bacterial or fungal infection, in which case you'll need to see your veterinarian.

Eye Care

Cleaning and examining the eyes should be a part of regular grooming, and by keeping your dog's eyes clean, you will be contributing to his overall health.

How to Care for Your Russell's Eyes

If a slight irritation appears, apply a commercial nonmedicated eyewash. Gently clean away any discharge that has gathered at the corners of the eye. If the discharge is yellow or green, and the eye is swollen or red, your dog needs veterinary care immediately. Do not wait.

To examine your dog's eyes, simply stroke him gently on the head, pulling back the ears—the eyes will naturally open wider and come clearly into view. A healthy dog's eyes should be wide open and bright. The center should be clear and shining, with pupils of the same size. The whites of the eyes should be pure white with no redness. Older dogs may have a greenish tinge to their eyes; this is a normal process of aging and nothing to worry about. The tissue beneath the lower lids should be a healthy pink, although some animals have a dark tinge on the membrane.

Paw Care

Don't neglect your Russell's paws, especially in winter. After all, he needs them to walk on!

How to Care for Your Russell's Paws

Keep the scraggly hair trimmed from between the paw pads, and in the winter, be scrupulous about cleaning salt from your dog's feet after a walk.

Trim your Russell's nails at least once a month. (If you can hear his toenails clicking on the floor, it's time.) Long nails can splay out the foot so badly that it becomes deformed. No matter how distasteful the process is to you or your dog, you must do it— unless you're lucky enough to have one of those dogs whose nails wear to the proper length by hitting the sidewalk.

You can use either scissors- or guillotine-type clippers—whichever you like best. Good-quality guillotine clippers have replaceable blades, which come in handy. Again, the key to successful clipping is early handling. If your dog isn't used to having his nails done, try playing with his feet at a time when he is comfortably relaxing. Use plenty of treats to make it a pleasant experience. If you can't get that far, start with his head and go very slowly down his leg. Don't rush the process.

If your dog really hates being bathed, try trimming his nails right before he gets a bath. Put him on the grooming table, and stand next to him facing his rear. (You can even put the dog in your lap if this is easier.) Begin with a back paw. Gently (but firmly) grasp each paw and press lightly to extend the nail. Clip the hooked tip at the same angle that it grows. Don't forget the dewclaws! Be sure to avoid the "quick," the living part of the nail that is usually visible through the white of the nail. If you mistakenly hit the quick, dab the spot with some styptic powder to stop the bleeding. If your dog objects to the process, try doing just a few nails at a time. If his nails are so bad that they must be trimmed immediately, have your groomer or vet do it. The last thing you want is to become the "bad guy" in your dog's eyes.

Some people (including me) have excellent luck using a cordless electric nail grinder on the nails. This tool

eliminates the possibility of splintering the nails and gives them a nice finish as well. Most dogs like nail grinding better than clipping once they get used to the noise and the odd feeling. The only caveat is that you should only use the grinder for a short time before letting it cool down.

Anal Sac Care

The anal sacs (often mistakenly called "glands") are two round organs located on each side of the anus at the 4 and 8 o'clock positions. They exude powerful,

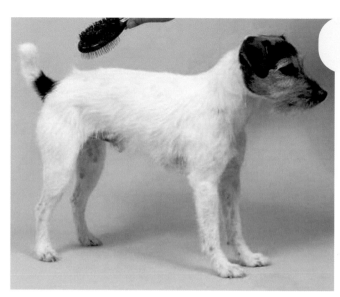

Daily grooming will help your dog look and feel his best.

- redness or swelling in the area, perhaps even an open, draining sore
- reluctance to sit
- scooting the rear end along the ground

How to Care for Your Russell's Anal Sacs

Some people recommend routine emptying of the anal sacs as a regular part of the grooming process, but this is not always a wise idea and can lead to further problems. If your dog doesn't exhibit the typical signs described here, then don't empty the anal sacs. It's not a very pleasant procedure, anyway.

If you suspect that your Russell's anal glands are impacted and want to try emptying them yourself, begin by holding a tissue up to anus and gently squeezing both sides. Squeeze the sacs between the thumb and forefingers into a tissue held just outside the anus. If the resulting secretion is paste-like, you probably won't be able to empty the sacs completely, and a trip to the vet may be in order.

A noninvasive measure that may help some dogs is to change to a high-fiber diet. This will produce a bulkier stool, which may help empty the anal

bad-smelling secretions that are used to give other dogs mating and territorial information. Every time a dog defecates, he deposits some of this material. Dogs can also empty their sacs when they are scared or overexcited. A few dogs, however, have difficulty expressing these sacs on their own.

Dogs of all breeds and of any age may encounter anal sac problems. Anal sacs can:

- become impacted or overfilled
- become infected with bacteria and even abscess
- develop tumors or harbor foreign bodies

Signs that your dog is encountering anal sac problems include:

- chewing or licking the tail base
- clamping the tail down over the anus
- difficulty in passing feces

sacs as it passes out through the rectum.

Dogs with a history of anal sac problems may be candidates for having them surgically removed. Because your dog doesn't really "need" them, this is a pretty benign procedure, although you must find a vet who is experienced with doing the operation. A careless mistake could injure the sphincter muscles.

Choosing a Professional Groomer

If you don't know a good groomer, ask for references from your vet or friends who have well-groomed dogs. When you have narrowed your search, call them and ask about their experience in grooming Russells, especially if your dog has a rough or broken coat. Don't make the beginning and end of the conversation "How much do you charge?" Specify what you want done, especially with regard to coat care and nail clipping. Also, ask what vaccinations are required before you go.

Make a visit to the shop to meet the staff. While they may be very busy, they should be friendly and pleasant. The shop should be clean, and tubs should be sterilized between every bath. If your dog must stay there for several hours, ask what arrangements they make for "potty breaks" for your dog. It's a good idea, by the way, not to feed your dog on the morning of his grooming appointment. If he's the nervous type, the strain might make him sick to his stomach. You should also exercise your dog before the visit so that he doesn't go crazy with boredom.

When your dog is properly groomed—brushed, washed, and with ears clean, nails trimmed, and eyes shining—it's time to show him off. Or maybe take him out in the woods for a run just to see how long it takes him to get dirty again. Remember, the Russell is a very natural dog who loves to play and get dirty in the great outdoors.

Controlling the Shed

Short-haired Russells are fairly heavy shedders. By nature, dogs shed most in the spring and fall, although I have to say that most Russells pay no attention to this rule and shed whenever they feel like it—which might be all year round. Frequent brushing helps keep shedding to a minimum.

Chapter 5

Feeling Good

Happiness and good health go paw in paw. The Russell is one of the hardiest of all breeds, but a little extra attention from you and his good friend the vet makes it even more certain that his life will be a long and comfortable one.

At your Russell's first vet visit, a nurse or vet tech will listen to his heart.

ask what special diagnostic services the clinic provides, such as ultrasound. Finally, it doesn't hurt to hang around outside the clinic and ask some outgoing clients how they like the vet.

The First Vet Visit

When you arrive at the vet's office, expect to fill out paperwork to start a medical record for your puppy, including his name, sex, age, and what veterinary care he has received already. A nurse or veterinary technician will weigh your puppy, take his temperature, and listen to his heart. When the vet comes in, she will probably ask you many questions about your puppy and also discuss plans for neutering him. During the exam itself, the vet will check the following:

- abdomen and navel
- eyes, ears, and teeth
- genitals
- heart and lungs
- joints
- skin

The Annual Vet Visit

Your dog should get regular checkups even when he is not exhibiting any signs of sickness. The yearly checkup should

Finding a Vet

Finding a good vet is not difficult, but it may take some time if you are a new dog owner.

First, please choose a vet who is close to your home. Five minutes more in travel time can make the difference between life and death. This doesn't necessarily mean that you should pick the closest vet if she is unsatisfactory, but it's a good place to start. Office hours are important, too, so check to see if they will fit into your schedule. Find out who handles emergencies after hours or on weekends. The staff should be friendly and knowledgeable, with a good "bedside manner"—and not just for your pet but for you as well. Ask about the vet's experience with Russells, and find out how familiar she is with their special needs. Also, be as thorough as the first one and may include a blood test for heartworm or other diagnostic procedures.

Vaccinations

When puppies are born, they receive special disease fighters called antibodies from their mothers' first milk, called the colostrum. The colostrum is almost as good as a vaccine to keep your puppy safe during his first few weeks. However, this passive immunity wears off, and your growing puppy soon needs vaccines to protect him.

Your dog requires regular vaccinations to stay healthy, but which ones he needs are partly determined by what region of the country you live in and what your dog's lifestyle is like. A country dog who charges around in tick-infested woods requires a different vaccine protocol than does a city slicker. And a dog who meets a lot of other dogs or who is kenneled frequently needs different vaccines than one who is the only dog on the block. Until your dog is fully vaccinated (at about four to six months of age), it's best to keep him away from situations in which he will be in contact with a lot of strange dogs.

Your veterinarian knows the right time for your puppy to be vaccinated; most vets do a series of vaccinations beginning between six and eight weeks of age.

Dogs are commonly vaccinated against all or some of the following:
- bordetella
- coronavirus
- distemper
- hepatitis
- leptospirosis
- Lyme disease
- parainfluenza
- parvovirus
- rabies

For a long time, dogs were automatically vaccinated every year. That policy has been re-evaluated, but we still don't know the duration of immunity for vaccines. Some, like bordetella, parainfluenza, and leptospirosis, may only give immunity for several months, while others may be good for several years. Talk to your vet about her booster protocol.

49

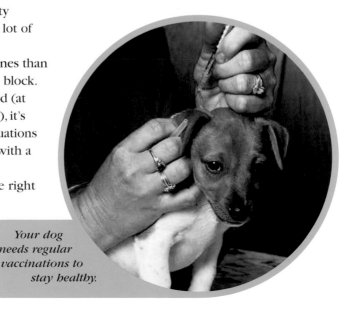

Your dog needs regular vaccinations to stay healthy.

Parasites

Parasites are creatures who make their living by feeding on your dog. Some exist on the outside of a dog (like fleas, mites, and ticks), while others (mostly worms and protozoa) live inside a dog. None of them are very pleasant, and some are even fatal.

External Parasites

External parasites live in a dog's hair or ears, and with the exception of some species of mites, they are usually visible.

Fleas

Fleas are external parasites who spend their entire adult lives on your dog, sucking blood and laying eggs. Flea eggs slide off an infested dog

when he scratches, and they become deposited where they fall and then hatch several days later. Three fleas can multiply to 10,000 fleas in three months, and they can easily infest your home.

Flea bites are irritating at best and can lead to severe itching and hair loss, especially at the base of the tail. A large infestation can cause serious anemia in puppies. To top it off, they cause all kinds of diseases, including plague, typhus, and tularemia. They also carry parasites such as tapeworm. Many dogs are so hypersensitive to flea saliva that they will itch all over from the bite of a single flea. This is called flea bite dermatitis.

A healthy dog is flea free, and prevention is the best way to accomplish this. Luckily, if your Russell is infested with fleas, you have a wide choice of safe flea killers. Some target adult fleas, while others are insect-growth inhibitors. Some are safe for puppies. Talk to your vet about the best choice for you.

Ticks

About 850 species of tick exist worldwide, causing everything from Rocky Mountain spotted fever to Lyme disease. Other tick-borne diseases include babesiosis, ehrlichiosis, tick paralysis, and tularemia.

Ticks are closely related to mites and spiders. They can't fly, but they possess a special organ that detects

FAMILY-FRIENDLY TIP

Visiting the Vet

If you bring your child along with you to your dog's first health exam, she will quickly learn what a great place the vet's office is and how good a friend the dog doctor is. Most vets are happy to explain what they are doing so that a child can understand the procedures and not be afraid of them. As an added bonus, visiting the vet may make your child less wary of her own pediatrician.

Check your Russell for fleas and ticks after he comes in from playing outdoors.

odor, heat, and humidity— in other words, a potential victim. To attack their prey, they climb up on tall grass and wait for their victim.

If you see a tick on your dog despite your best efforts, remove it right away. Use tweezers or a special tick-removal instrument that grabs the tick without squeezing it and causing it to reinject its fluids back into your dog. Don't touch the tick with your bare hands. Grasp it with the tweezers as close to its head as you can, and pull it straight out. Clean the wound with disinfectant, and then wash your hands. Throw the tick in the toilet and flush it down. After you remove the tick, you may notice some redness and swelling at the site of the bite. This is a reaction to the tick's saliva, but it does not mean the tick's head is embedded in the wound. That very seldom happens, actually.

Mites

Several species of mites also live on your dog, including the following:

- **Cheyletiella mites:** These mites are the nicest of the lot because they don't actually do any damage. They look like tiny little spiders under a microscope and are often referred to as walking dandruff. You can easily get rid of them by using any common flea shampoo. Be careful, though—these mites are contagious to humans.
- **Sarcoptic mites:** These mites cause scabies, signs of which include extreme itching, hair loss, and inflammation. Sarcoptic mites are difficult to detect by skin scrapings, because they can burrow deep into the skin. In fact, veterinarians often treat for them if they suspect their presence because it's so hard to get a good diagnosis.
- **Demodex mites:** These mites live and reproduce just under the skin's surface in tiny hair follicles and oil glands. They are easily viewed with

a skin scraping, unlike scabies mites. Demodex is most commonly seen in puppies, and if present in older dogs, may be a sign that the immune system is overstressed. Demodex mites do not cause as much itching as scabies, but dogs can still lose their hair. Medication is available.

Internal Parasites

Dogs are prey to many types of internal parasites, and they are dangerous because they can do a lot of damage before you even realize that your pet is infested with them. This is why it's so important to keep your dog on a year-round parasite preventive.

Internal parasites can cause problems such as diarrhea, weight loss, anemia, and vomiting. The following are some common internal parasites:

- giardia
- heartworm
- hookworm
- ringworm (despite the name, ringworm is a fungal infection)
- roundworm
- tapeworm
- whipworm

Breed-Specific Health Issues in Russells

Although Russell Terriers are, for the most part, extremely healthy dogs, they may be predisposed to a few diseases. This doesn't mean that they

Neutering Your Russell Terrier

All pet dogs should be neutered, preferably before the age of six months. In males, the medical benefits of neutering include eliminating or vastly reducing the risk of perineal hernias, penile tumors, and testicular or prostate cancers; in females, mammary cancers can be prevented. Dogs who have been neutered are less inclined to wander, mark, and behave aggressively.

are at a high risk for them, or even that they are more predisposed than are other dogs; it just means that some lines of Russell have a slightly greater-than-average chance of acquiring them.

Cataracts

Hereditary cataracts are reported in more than 60 dog breeds, and the Russell Terrier is one of the breeds most commonly affected. A cataract is any abnormal cloudiness of the eye lens, a transparent structure that lies directly behind the iris and pupil. The

First-Aid Kits for Dogs

Keep the following items in your canine first-aid kit to ensure that you are prepared for an emergency:

- 3% hydrogen peroxide (to induce vomiting)
- activated charcoal (for poisoning)
- aloe vera (for minor burns)
- antibiotic cream
- antibiotic soap (skin and wound cleanser)
- baking soda (for burns caused by acids)
- bandages
- Benadryl (1–2 mg per lb [0.5 kg] every 8 hours; two to four 25-mg tablets every 8 hours)
- Betadine (for treating wounds)
- canine first-aid manual
- canine rectal thermometer
- clinging wrap heat or ice pack
- Epsom salts (for soaking wounds, especially on the feet)
- eye dropper
- gauze and cotton pads (to clean and cover wounds)
- gentle eye wash formulated for dogs
- hydrocortisone cream (for minor inflammation)
- Imodium or Kaopectate for diarrhea (1 mg per 15 lbs [6.8 kg] one or two times a day, or 1 tbsp (14.8 ml) for every 10 lbs [4.5 kg] every 6 hours.)
- magnifying glass
- milk of magnesia (for constipation, administer with equal amounts of mineral oil)
- mineral oil (for numerous uses, including to relieve constipation)
- Pepto-Bismol (for digestive upsets and diarrhea; 1 tsp (4.9 ml) per 5 lbs [2.3 kg] during a 6-hour period)
- petroleum jelly
- round tip scissors
- rubber or latex gloves (to protect your hands and prevent contamination of wounds)
- saline eye solution and artificial tear gel
- soft muzzle (injured dogs tend to bite)
- styptic powder (stops minor bleeding)
- syringe (without needle) or turkey baster (to administer oral medication)
- thermal blanket (prevents shock by preserving a dog's body heat)
- tweezers or hemostat
- vinegar (for burns caused by alkaloids)
- witch hazel (for insect bites, minor injuries)

cataract may be a tiny spot, or it may cover a large part of the eye.

Inherited canine cataracts typically afflict young adults and can often develop slowly over a period of years. Other causes include diabetes, infection, shock, and eye trauma. In early stages, vision is not affected, but as time goes on, the dog may lose sight in the eye. (Or he may not—not all cataracts progress to a state of blindness.) You may not even notice that your Russell has a cataract until he starts bumping into furniture. In many cases, surgery, especially when performed early, can restore vision. The surgical procedure, called phacoemulsification, involves the ultrasonic destruction of the lens. Your dog can see quite well without the lens,

but he won't be able to focus properly. Still, it's better than being blind.

Cerebellar Ataxia

This inherited nervous disorder results from degeneration of the cerebellum's cortex. Affected dogs typically have a wobbly gait and seem disoriented. No cure is available, unfortunately, but breeders are working to eliminate the problem.

Congestive Heart Failure

Congestive heart failure (CHF), a condition to which Russells are prone, is usually caused by a leaky heart valve. Like the human heart, a dog's heart has four valves. When a problem occurs with one of them, the dog develops a heart murmur. Some dogs are born with a valvular problem, while others can acquire it later in life, perhaps from a bacterial infection. The other cause of CHF is cardiomyopathy, a condition characterized by a weak heart muscle. In severe cases, the lungs fill with water, causing weakness or even sudden death during exercise. This is why it's important to have your dog's health checked regularly by a professional and also to watch your pet carefully for signs of distress, such as labored breathing.

Early signs of CHF include coughing, wheezing, difficulty breathing, and weight

A big change in appetite could mean that your dog isn't feeling well.

loss. Dogs with CHF should be on a low-salt diet and receive regular professional care. All medications, such as diuretics and ACE inhibitors, should be administered on schedule. The outlook depends on how severe the disease is in your dog.

Cruciate Ligament Rupture

Highly athletic dogs like the Russell Terrier are extremely prone to getting this kind of injury. A ligament is a tough tissue connecting two bones—in this case, in the knee. If the ligament tears, it allows the thighbone to slide back and forth over the shin bone. It causes not only pain but also (later) arthritis. In a few cases, the rupture repairs itself with rest, but in the majority of cases, the dog needs surgery. All surgical cases usually involve entering the joint and cleaning out ligament remnants as well as damaged cartilage and joint surfaces. Afterward, the dog's activity must be restricted for two months.

High Toes or Short Toes

In this curious condition, usually the toes of the front feet are shorter than normal. It doesn't really affect a dog negatively,

The Expert Knows

Pet Insurance

If you haven't noticed already, vet care can get pretty pricey, not because the vets are making fortunes but because new, high-tech treatments that were once reserved only for humans are now available for dogs, including radiation therapy, hip replacements, and kidney transplants. Although currently only about 3 percent of pet owners have health insurance for their animals, it may be a good idea for you, especially if you are not good at saving money. Pet insurance companies work pretty much like human ones, charging premiums and offering deductibles, exclusions, and different levels of coverage. Check with your vet about whether or not this might be a good option for you.

but it does look odd. This is considered a serious defect for show dogs.

Legg-Calve-Perthes Disease

This disease is an inherited degeneration of the head of the thigh bone that causes progressive rear leg lameness. It usually doesn't show up until a puppy is at least four months old, and Russell Terriers are considered at a higher risk for this condition than many other breeds. The disease is usually treated surgically with a procedure in which part of the thighbone is removed. The prognosis is very good, especially if combined with physical therapy soon after surgery.

Feeling Good

Help keep your Russell healthy by making sure that he gets plenty of exercise.

Lens Luxation

Lens luxation is a fairly common inherited disease in Russells. In this condition, one or both eye lenses become dislocated from their normal location behind the cornea. If the luxation is complete, the lens will be painful, and the eye will look red or opaque. The condition usually shows up in older dogs and must be treated right away to avoid blindness.

General Illnesses

As a rule, Russell Terriers are extremely healthy dogs, having far fewer inherited defects than do most breeds. However, a dog can become ill from any number of causes, so consult your vet if your dog shows signs of any of the general disorders described in this section.

Abscessed Teeth

The last premolar tooth of the upper jaw often becomes infected and abscessed. Because this tooth has three very long roots, the swelling may extend into the surrounding bone and break through the skin, appearing as a draining wound below the eye. Your vet will likely remove the tooth.

Allergies

Just as people do, animals suffer from allergies. And while people are apt to sneeze or get a runny nose, allergies usually show up in dogs as a skin problem. In fact, one kind of allergy, called contact dermatitis, is an allergic skin reaction that actually occurs on the thin-skinned areas of the body that actually come into contact with the allergen, like the abdomen and lower chest. Most of the time, though, dogs get a kind of allergy called atopy, an allergy to pollen, mold, or dust mites that float through the air.

Tests for allergies can be complicated and not always reliable, and the disorder is usually lifelong. Treatment is designed only to relieve the signs, not cure the disease. In any case, the best procedure is to remove the allergen from the dog's environment if possible. If that won't work, routine bathing is helpful, as is anti-inflammatory medication prescribed by your vet.

Arthritis

Although we tend to think of arthritis as affecting only older canines, dogs of any age can be affected. Arthritis can strike anywhere, with the hips, elbows, knees, backs, and necks representing the most common sites. Some kinds of arthritis are referred to as degenerative, meaning that it comes from problems in the joint itself; another kind, called inflammatory, may be the result of a disease like Lyme disease.

Early signs of arthritis include a reluctance to climb and jump. And

because these signs can also signal very serious problems, like a ruptured disk, it's important to get your dog checked over by your vet, who will look for swelling, pain, and decreased range of motion. She may order an X-ray to look for bone changes or even do a joint tap to check the synovial fluid that lubricates the joints.

Although no cure is available, a variety of helpful treatments exist, such as anti-inflammatory medication, especially if arthritis is diagnosed early. Mild exercise may also help. If your dog is overweight, you will be told to put him on a diet, because obese dogs put increased pressure on the joints. If no medication helps, surgery may be recommended; bone fragments can be removed, and in some cases, the whole joint can be removed. This sounds bad, but small, tough, well-muscled dogs like Russells are ideal candidates for this kind of surgery.

Bumps and Lumps

Dogs may develop odd bumps and lumps from time to time, and they could be anything from harmless cysts to cancer. Not even a veterinarian can tell what a lump is just by looking at it. When presented with a lump, your vet has two options: She can perform a fine needle biopsy and examine the cells under a microscope, or she can remove the lump surgically and examine the cells. What option your vet chooses depends on a variety of factors, including your dog's history, the appearance of the lump, and the location of the lump. Never ignore a lump, especially one that appears suddenly, seems attached to the bone, or is growing rapidly.

Canine Cognitive Dysfunction

Canine cognitive dysfunction is an age-related deterioration of your dog's thinking ability. It is sometimes called old dog syndrome or senility. Signs include aimless wandering, loss of housetraining, getting "stuck" behind furniture or in corners, and similar signs of dementia. In addition, affected dogs may appear withdrawn and uninterested in being petted. Consult your vet if you suspect that your dog may be suffering from canine cognitive dysfunction; medical treatments do exist for this condition.

Cushing's Disease (Hyperadrenocortism)

The adrenal glands of dogs with Cushing's disease produce too much cortisol, a hormone with strong anti-inflammatory and immuno-suppressive effects. Some dogs inherit the disease, but most dogs get it because of a

tumor on the pituitary or adrenal glands. A third form can develop if the dog is given steroids without being properly weaned off them.

This disease is usually seen in middle-aged and older dogs. Signs include hair loss, excessive drinking and urination, exercise intolerance, a pot-bellied abdomen, and chronic nfections. Several medications can help affected dogs maintain a quality of life.

Diabetes

Several hundred thousand dogs are estimated to have diabetes. It can occur at any age but is most often diagnosed between the ages of seven and nine. Diabetes mellitus is caused by a deficiency of insulin, a hormone produced by certain cells in the

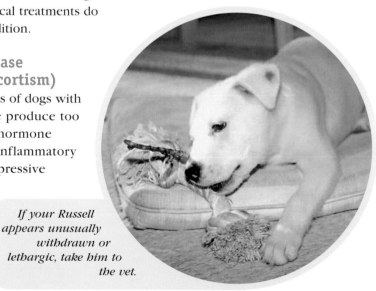

If your Russell appears unusually withdrawn or lethargic, take him to the vet.

pancreas. Without insulin, sugar remains in the bloodstream and passes into the urine. This, in turn, causes increased urine production and thirst. Hunger also increases because the body can't use the sugar in the blood, and so the dog is always hungry. (Sugar makes you feel full, which is why a candy bar before dinner spoils the appetite.) As diabetes progresses, chemicals called ketones accumulate, resulting in vomiting and dehydration. Unless the dog is treated, he will die. Females are twice as likely to get diabetes, and so they should be spayed and monitored carefully for urinary tract infections.

Diabetes is not curable, but with proper insulin administration, it can be controlled. Most of the time, this kind of diabetes can't be managed by diet alone and will require the owner to administer one to two injections of insulin a day for the rest of the dog's life. Diabetic dogs are usually put on a diet of frequent small meals as well.

Ear Infections

Ear infections are one of the most serious problems of dogs. The microorganisms that cause it (yeast, bacteria, and fungi) just love the warm, dark, moist environment of the ear. Pathogens can get into a Russell's ear when he swims, when it rains, or when he digs through the dirt in search of who knows what. In fact, nature probably couldn't design a

SENIOR DOG TIP
Your Aging Russell

Older dogs generally have great genes—that's how they managed to hang in there that long! Of course, your older Russell may be a bit slower and stiffer than he used to be, and some older dogs become blind or deaf. Oddly, owners are more disturbed by their pet's declining health than the dogs seem to be. Dogs are infinite pragmatists, and you'll find that if you provide them with good vet care, grooming, moderate, regular exercise, regular meals, and plenty of love, then both of you will enjoy several truly golden years together.

better bacteria incubator than a dog's ear canals. The inside of a dog's ears are an extension of his skin, of course, but unlike the tough terrier skin of the outer body, the delicate ear canal lining is thin and easily torn and inflamed.

Your role as a wise dog owner is to check your Russell's ears frequently and make sure that they are clean. Call your vet if you see any signs of a problem, such as redness, swelling, or itchiness. In most cases, antibiotics, ear flushing, or allergy medications will resolve the issue, although in a few serious cases, surgery may be required.

Lenticular (Nuclear) Sclerosis

This is a very common and normal age-related change to the eye, often seen in dogs past the age of seven years. The cloudiness you see is probably a result of increased insoluble proteins in the lens. Dogs who are exposed to a lot of sunlight are the most likely victims. The sclerosis doesn't significantly affect vision, but it superficially resembles a cataract. A veterinarian must examine the dog to tell the difference.

Pericardial Disease

The pericardium is a sac that surrounds the heart. The most common disease affecting it is pericardial effusion (fluid in the sac). This may result from infection, congestive heart failure, hemorrhage, or cancer. Signs include muffled or displaced heart sounds, vomiting, and difficulty breathing. Therapy involves removing the fluid through a needle placed into the sac. Surgery may also be needed.

Emergencies

Accidents happen, and they seem particularly likely to happen with dogs

The Russell's small size makes him vulnerable to hypothermia, so limit his time outdoors in very cold temperatures.

who are energetic, curious, and fearless, like the Russell. Your role is to prevent what you can, and if you can't be prepared, to take immediate, calm action if an emergency arises.

Hypothermia

If your Russell is left outside in winter without shelter, he could become a victim of hypothermia. Hypothermia is a condition in which body temperature drops too low for the body to function normally; if it becomes too low, the temperature will not return to normal without treatment, even after the animal is put in a warm room. Although the Russell's fur protects him to some degree, his small size also makes him vulnerable. Signs of hypothermia include violent shivering and slow, shallow breathing. The tissues can also become damaged.

To treat a hypothermic dog, warm him slowly. You can wrap him in a warm blanket or towels. (warm them by putting them in the dryer). Or fill plastic bottles with warm (not hot) water, and place them in the groin and armpit areas. If the dog is also wet, dry him gently with a hair dryer. During the warming process, call your vet and discuss whether or not he should be brought in for evaluation. As your dog starts to recover, keep him hydrated by giving him water with some honey or sugar in it.

Heatstroke

Dogs are wonderful creatures, but they have a major defect. They can't sweat. They have to cool off by panting, which is not very efficient. In extreme heat, a dog can easily go into life-threatening cardiovascular shock. Puppies and older dogs are most susceptible. Signs

of heatstroke include:

• bright red tongue
• dark red or very pale gums
• erratic breathing
• sluggishness

If you suspect hypothermia, get your dog into the shade and immerse or spray him with cool water. Do not use ice or freezing cold water—these will constrict your Russell's blood vessels and trap the heat inside his body. Keep taking his temperature, and stop cooling him down when his temperature reaches 103°F (39.4°C). At this point, take him to the vet.

It should come as no surprise that most dogs with heatstroke were affected while trapped inside a hot car. It is not enough to leave the windows open. Never leave a dog in the car when the temperature is over 60°F (15.6°C) or if your car is parked in the sun.

Poisons

Do not assume that your Russell will exercise caution in his eating habits. Dogs are natural scavengers, and what you find repulsive may seem like the most delicious meal to them. As a result, it's important to keep dangerous items away from your dog and be on the alert for signs of poisoning such as vomiting, diarrhea, staggering, or disorientation.

Never leave your Russell in a hot vehicle.

tablespoons [44.4 to 59.1 ml] of it can kill a Russell.) Obviously, dogs who are allowed to wander around the neighborhood are most at risk, as are dogs who are confined in (or allowed access to) the garage, where they can lick it off the floor.

Dogs are extremely attracted to the smell and taste of this stuff, so it is critically important that you keep it away from your dog and mop up any spills. Store antifreeze in clearly marked containers, and check your vehicle for leaks. If possible, use products that do not contain ethylene glycol. Also, don't let your Russell drink from puddles, because the water runoff may contain antifreeze from neighborhood cars. Wash his paws after taking him for a walk, and of course, never let your dog roam free.

Poisonous Foods

Many people foods may be toxic or otherwise unsafe for dogs. These include alcohol, avocado, chocolate, coffee, tea, garlic, grapes, macadamia nuts, onions, raisins, and yeast dough. Fruit pits can also cause damage, as can tomato leaves or stems.

Antifreeze

Every year, almost 10,000 dogs and cats are victims of accidental poisoning from antifreeze. A dog doesn't need to drink much to ingest a fatal dose. (Most commercial antifreeze consists mainly of ethylene glycol, and only 3 to 4

Toxic Plants

Many ornamental outdoor plants, like lily-of-the-valley, daffodils, rhododendron, and hydrangea, are poisonous to dogs. And although adult dogs are seldom attracted to such things, puppies will eat anything. Signs can range from stomach upset to convulsions or death.

Alternative Therapies

Although standard Western medicine is the bedrock of health care, at times other options may be extremely beneficial as well.

Acupuncture

Acupuncture involves the use of fine needles to stimulate certain points of the nerves to get energy (or as the Chinese call it, chi) flowing again. The treatment is usually painless. Acupuncture has been shown to have therapeutic effect in a wide variety of canine diseases, both for pain management and the treatment of various structural and functional disorders. It is most popularly used for back problems, especially back problems due to trauma. Some vets even use it as a diagnostic aid. It can be used in combination with other methods of treatment, although it should not be used on pregnant animals. Some drugs, such as tranquilizers, steroids, or anticonvulsive drugs, can also diminish its effects. For some conditions, only one treatment is necessary. Carefully observe your dog following each treatment.

Herbal Therapy

Herbs are the basis of many modern drugs, so it makes sense that the herbs themselves can be used to treat various illnesses. Herbalists claim that because they use whole herbs unaltered by chemical additions, rather than extracts of one component of the herb, they achieve better healing.

Veterinarians skilled in their use prescribe herbs in the same way that they do conventional drugs. Be aware, though, that many herbs can be dangerous if used incorrectly. It is very important not to experiment with this kind of therapy on your own but to see a holistic veterinarian.

Homeopathy

Homeopathy is a therapy developed by a German physician, Samuel Hahnemann, in the early 1800s. Hahnemann considered disease to be a disruption in the life force, and he believed that the body could be stimulated into healing itself. His idea relied on the age-old *Law of Similars*, or "like cures like." In other words, he believed that to cure an

illness, you should give the patient a very small, diluted amount of a substance that in large amounts would produce symptoms similar to the target disease.

Homeopathic medicines are natural substances prepared by a process of serial dilution and succession, or repeated shaking. The final product has been diluted from ten times to millions of times. Although no scientific evidence has shown homeopathy to work, many people swear by its effects, and some holistic veterinarians use homeopathic remedies to treat animals.

Massage

One popular natural therapy is massage, which is not only soothing but actually heals. Massage involves applying pressure to specific parts of the body. The average massage session is 30 minutes. A well-done massage reduces

stress, decreases pain, improves flexibility, and increases circulation. It may also remove toxins from the body. However, it is not a substitute for veterinary care and should not be used on animals with fever, shock, infection, rashes, or open wounds.

Flower Essence Therapy

In the early 1930s, English physician Dr. Edward Bach developed a system of therapy that depended on flowers, which he considered to have healing powers, especially for conditions that originate in the emotions. Today, many flower remedies exist, and they are available at any health food store.

The most important part of flower essence therapy is to match the right essence with your dog's personality type. Submissive, abused dogs who tremble and keep their heads down, for instance, are said to benefit from aspen

Active dogs can benefit from massage therapy.

and larch. No double-blind studies show that these essences actually work on dogs, but they may give their owners more confidence, and that alone is enough to show that they can be of some benefit.

Flower essences can be used with other methods of treatment. In fact, these safe remedies contain no chemical substances with harmful side effects, although the preservative (often alcohol) conceivably could be harmful.

The End

All good things come to an end in time, and saying goodbye is the hardest part of owning a pet. If your dog is suffering from a painful terminal illness, it is important to talk to your vet about euthanasia in advance. You will often know it is "time" when your dog no longer seems to enjoy eating or doing other things that used to make him happy. Many terminally ill dogs no longer seem to respond to their owners, almost as if they are telling them that the time to say goodbye has come.

When the time has come, decide whether or not you wish to be present. Your Russell will understand either way. You are not abandoning him, especially if you are so upset that your emotions may be stressful to him. Of course, if you wish to be present, and you feel that you can support your dog, that is the right decision for you.

Be assured that euthanasia is painless and quick (less than five seconds). The vet first inserts a needle or

Good preventive care will help your Russell lead a happy, active life.

catheter into a leg vein, and she may then inject a drug that will make your dog very relaxed. She then administers the drug itself, which causes the heart to stop beating. Although in some cases involuntary muscle movement occurs, your pet no longer feels anything but peace.

Give yourself and your family permission to mourn the passing of your dear friend, but don't lock up your heart forever. I can assure you that the day will come when a certain pair of bright eyes capture your heart all over again.

Chapter 6

Being Good

Dogs are always learning, and they soak up information like sponges. What they learn, however, depends on you. Every time you interact with your dog, whether intentionally or unintentionally, he is learning. Your dog can learn to be a well-behaved, obedient, responsive joy, or a frightened, willful, disobedient horror. The choice is yours.

lthough training takes some time and a little effort, you will find it an energizing, bonding, and even fun experience. And its rewards are immense!

Why Is Training Important?

A trained dog is joy to be around. He makes a delightful family member, a polite houseguest, and an interesting companion. Untrained dogs are noisy, pesky, and a danger to themselves and to others. The best way to avoid these problems is to make yourself and your dog happy by training him the right way right away.

Socialization

Socialization is one of the most important gifts that you can give your Russell. A well-socialized dog is neither fearful of nor aggressive toward strangers. Unsocialized dogs, on the other hand, can turn into fear biters and may pick fights with other dogs. This is why your Russell should meet as many new people in as many different circumstances as possible. In fact, the sooner you begin this training, the more successful you will be!

To socialize your dog, have him meet a variety of people of all ages, races, and of both sexes. Let him get used to their carrying boxes, umbrellas, and vacuum cleaners. Move stuff around your house as well, putting familiar objects in unfamiliar locations and positions—the kitchen chair on its side in the living room, for example. You should both invite people to your home to meet the dog and also take him all to the places where dogs are allowed, so that he becomes used to

Socialize your dog to a variety of different people and animals.

different kinds of environments. Take him for frequent car rides. He should also get used to all kinds of different sounds, including the vacuum cleaner. But start slowly; don't suddenly blast an unsuspecting puppy with the full force of the vacuum cleaner.

In addition, socialization can help your dog become accustomed to being groomed and handled. This includes ear cleaning, brushing, bathing, and nail clipping. This is also the time to get him used to his collar and leash. Be cheerful and upbeat, and don't attempt to overly restrain your dog. Keep the sessions short, and end on a positive note!

Crate Training

Crates are wonderful things. They help with housetraining, protect the dog from ill-behaved children, and keep him safe when you can't supervise him. And just as important, the crate provides a nice, safe place for him to sleep.

The easiest way to train your dog to use the crate is to simply start feeding him his dinner in it—with the door open. In about a minute, the crate will become his favorite place. If you have the rare dog who just

Finding a Trainer

Although many people effectively train their dogs at home, others do best with the structure and companionship of a formal obedience class. The ideal time to begin is between 12 and 16 weeks, when your Russell has had his necessary vaccinations and has been certified as healthy by your veterinarian. If you have a puppy, a puppy kindergarten class will also teach him the basics of socialization, one of the most important lessons of all.

Don't select a trainer at random—get recommendations from trusted friends, veterinarians, or kennel club members. Check the trainer's credentials, because many of the good ones are members of a professional organization such as the Association of Pet Dog Trainers (APDT). And visit a few classes without your dog. Participants (both human and canine) should seem relaxed, enthusiastic, and comfortable. Look for lots of smiling. Does the trainer seem interested in listening as well as talking? That's important. And because the training is as much for you as for your dog, work with someone with whom you have rapport. The most effective trainers use positive reinforcement rather than punishment, so pay attention to how the dogs are being asked to do what is required. And of course, the facility should be safe and clean.

doesn't like a crate and whines while in it, don't give in by letting him out the minute he whimpers. Hold fast until he is quiet, and then let him out.

Some rescue dogs have been brutally confined to cages past the point of endurance. These animals may exhibit what is called "cage rage" and repeatedly fling themselves against the walls. In this case, you may have to avoid crates altogether or be ready to take a very, very long time getting him used to one.

Housetraining

Because your Russell is going to share your home, it's pretty important that he not use it as his toilet. But that's what is going to happen unless you take steps to teach him to use the great outdoors.

Housetraining Methods

You can use a variety of methods to housetrain your dog, including paper training, housetraining with a crate, and housetraining by constant supervision. No matter what kind of training you use, though, it helps to give your dog some verbal cues to let him know what you want. When you see his pre-elimination pattern, for example, say "Outside!" in a cheerful voice, and carry him out. The closer to the door you are when you say this, the better, but your puppy won't always cooperate. Once outside, use another verbal cue to get him to perform the behavior, such as "Hurry up!" Do praise

your puppy when he does the right thing. Help your dog learn to associate where to eliminate. Don't simply put your dog outside and abandon him. He must learn that he has a "mission." Take your dog to the chosen area on a leash.

Some trainers say that it's vital to take the dog inside right away after he eliminates so that he identifies the commands with elimination and doesn't mistake the potty trip for a regular walk or playtime. This is important when you are in a hurry and don't have time before work for a romp. On the other hand, some dogs attempt to hold it as long as possible if they know they are being returned to the house immediately, so I think it's a good idea to add a little playtime to the trip after the dog succeeds, even if it's only for a minute or two.

Paper Training

In so-called "paper training," you place papers (or nowadays, pretreated pads) on the floor in a particular spot and encourage the dog to use that place. You do this by watching the puppy carefully, and when he begins the "bathroom dance," which may include circling and sniffing, you pick him up and gently take him to the desired spot. When he succeeds, praise him wildly. To transition your puppy to using the great outdoors, you can place the papers closer and closer to the door and then remove them entirely.

Although this training method is

rather out of fashion these days, it's a lifesaver when you are gone from home for a large part of the day. Think of the peace of mind you will have knowing that your puppy is using his pads, not the Oriental carpet.

The Crate

The second method of housetraining involves the use of a crate. Whenever the puppy is inside the home but cannot be supervised, put him in the crate. He will soon learn that he can "hold it" when necessary. Using too big a crate may create long-term problems, because the pup can simply use one corner of it to eliminate. Then, he'll track it through the whole crate, and pretty soon his natural instinct to keep his bedding area clean will be impossible to obey. Eventually, it will be forgotten entirely. It is your job, of course, to make sure that he gets out to do his business before those first promptings become a screaming necessity. The first thing you do in the morning is to make a trip outdoors. At night, the last thing you should do before you put the puppy in the crate is take him outside to his appointed place.

Supervision

Another method of housetraining simply involves constant supervision. If you are home all day and have the ability to keep your puppy next to you all his waking hours for a few days, you can simply watch him like a hawk, and the instant you see him go into his pre-elimination pattern, rush him outdoors.

Accidents

Never punish your puppy for making a mistake. If an accident happens and you missed it, it's too late. Even if it only happened half a minute ago, your puppy has forgotten all about it. You simply need to clean it up without comment. If you do catch him in the act, pick him up and say "Outside" as before.

When your puppy shows signs that he has to eliminate, take him outside immediately.

Prevent poor leash manners by teaching your Russell to walk nicely beside you.

even with a newspaper, and never "rub his nose in it." This kind of punishment will simply convince your dog that the best thing to do is not to be caught, and he will soon start hiding his waste.

Obedience Training

Even though your dog doesn't have to be Lassie, he should be able to obey basic obedience commands. Basic training will enable you to control your dog. This will keep him safe, reduce the "nuisance factor," and make him a pleasant companion and welcome guest.

Watch Me

The very first thing that your puppy must learn is to pay attention to you, which he will learn with the *watch me* command. This helps your dog learn to focus on you rather than on distractions. Learning the command also teaches him to read your face, a skill at which dogs can become unnervingly good. Also, if you teach your dog to pay attention now, all other command training will be easier.

How to Teach Watch Me

You can get your dog to pay attention by squeaking a toy or using a clicker behind your ear. Offer a treat when he looks up, and soon you'll have an adoring pup watching your every

While you are carrying him, push his tail down to keep him from continuing while he's in your arms. Always praise him when he finishes correctly, and vow to watch over him more carefully in the future. Never strike your dog,

frightened) when someone stares at them, a dominant dog may stare back and growl. Eventually, most dogs get used to the idea that the fact that you're staring at them doesn't really mean that you want a confrontation. However, most dogs are more comfortable if you just stare at the tip of their ears if you must look at them.

Although dog are perfectly capable of understanding many spoken words, body language conveys infinitely more information to them. In fact, your tone of voice, eye contact, posture, and the way in which you handle a dog are full of meaning to him.

Voice Tone

Speak in a clear tone. If your dog is shy or frightened, speak gently. If he is strong and dominant, speak firmly.

Eye Contact

Eye contact is probably the most important element of body language. In the dog world, a stare is a challenge. Although most dogs naturally look away (or even urinate on the ground if really

Posture

A tall, upright position exudes confidence to a dog. If you have a shy or frightened pet, you can comfort him by bowing your head or even crouching down to his level. On the other hand, sitting on the floor with a dominant dog may convince him that you are subservient to him. In this case, stand tall, speak deeply, and mean what you say.

Handling

Many dogs are sensitive about having their muzzle or the nape of their neck handled. It probably reminds them of when they were young and their mother grabbed them by the neck and shook them if they misbehaved. Because of this, hugging a dog around the neck and kissing him may evoke an aggressive response. It's important not to allow children to do this, either.

expression. Do not offer the treat first! You want him looking at you, not searching for the treat.

Polite Walking

Walking a polite dog on a leash is a relaxing yet energizing activity. Being tangled in a leash, tripping along after a lunging dog, or dragging along a dog who wants to go elsewhere is not. Fortunately, teaching your Russell to walk politely on a leash will go a long way toward preventing these problems.

How to Teach Polite Walking

To teach your Russell how to walk politely on leash, first get a 12- to 15-foot (3.7- to 4.6-m) nonretractable lead and a whole bunch of high-value treats. (A high-value treat is something that your dog loves more than anything else.) Take your dog to an area that he knows well and that is quiet, with few distractions. You want him to focus on you, not other dogs or people. Then, attach the leash, say "Walkies" in a cheerful tone, and start walking.

The biggest problem people have with walking their dog is that he pulls or lunges forward on the leash. Walking such a dog is no fun at all, but you can do a few things to solve the problem. Most dogs pull or lunge because they are overexcited at the prospect of a walk,

especially if they see other dogs or children approaching from the opposite direction. If that happens, you can turn your Russell in the opposite direction. Use tiny, fingernail-sized treats to reward him for paying attention to you, not the distraction. Always pay attention to your dog and praise him for focusing on you and following you. Don't reward his willfulness or excitement with any verbal cues, not even a "no." Say nothing at all and do nothing until he does what you want. This is particularly important if your dog shows aggression toward other dogs. After several instances of being turned around in the opposite direction, your Russell will pick up the hint to walk quietly.

An alternative method is to simply have your dog sit down quietly when a stranger approaches. Pet him gently, and praise him for being quiet. If he likes children, allow them to pet him, but don't let your active terrier jump up on a strange child. If you are not certain how your dog will react to a stranger, don't allow him to be petted. Whatever you do, don't allow the dog to be in charge of the walk by following *him*.

Come

A well-trained dog comes on command. This is not merely a matter of courtesy—it can also save his life if he is engaged in a dangerous behavior, such as if he is chasing a squirrel into oncoming traffic, for example.

How to Teach Come

To start teaching this behavior, use a leash. Some people never practice calling their dog until they are outside and the dog is off-lead and having fun. This gives him the perfect opportunity not to obey and still get a reward (continued fun in the sun) for disobedience. Even if he does come the first time that you call, what is his reward? Being put on a leash and taken home! The intelligent Russell soon learns it pays better not to obey, especially if, as sometimes happens, the owner punishes the dog when he eventually returns. Soon he learns that the word "come" means "stay away for as long as possible."

A special word here, though. You have a breed with a strong prey drive. Situations will inevitably occur in which your dog encounters a distraction of such high value that literally nothing you can do will prevent him from running off. Most Russells would rather chase a squirrel or cat than eat a steak dinner. That's why we have leashes. Until your dog will reliably come to you whenever you call while he is leashed, he should not be permitted to run loose.

When you start training, pick a time when your dog is fairly hungry and will respond eagerly to food treats. From the very beginning, you want him to associate obeying you with good things. Start by letting him know that you have food and then back up, saying "Come!" Most puppies respond eagerly, but some older dogs who have had bad experiences may be reluctant to heed the command. With these dogs, you need to offer extremely tasty treats, like pea-sized bits of cheese or liver, and wait until they are hungry. After your dog gets the idea, you can begin to omit the food rewards some of the time and replace them with praise or petting. Intermittent rewards actually work better than consistent rewards to assure good behavior. Eventually, you should be able to get it down to one food reward for every five successful completions of the *come* command.

When your dog comes to you reliably, add another person to the game. Each person should stand at opposite ends of the room, and each should call the dog, rewarding him once in a while. Only the person calling the dog should give the treat. Dogs love this, and they learn fast.

As your dog becomes more and more proficient, add distractions of increased levels of intensity. Finally, attempt all these exercises off-lead once your dog comes reliably. If your dog makes a mistake, go back to on-leash training until he has it right.

Sit

The point of this exercise is to have your dog situated with his rear end on the floor and his head up looking expectantly at you. A sitting dog is quiet, relatively immobile, and usually paying more attention to his trainer than one who is wandering around on his own.

How to Teach Sit

As always, begin in a distraction-free room when your Russell is hungry. While he is standing, hold a high-value treat close to his nose and then move it slowly over his head toward the back. He will naturally sit. (Do not push his hind end to the floor in an attempt to force him to sit—this is not

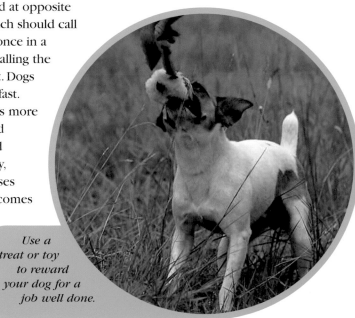

Use a treat or toy to reward your dog for a job well done.

necessary.) The instant he sits, praise him and give him the treat. As with the *come* lesson, after your Russell is proficient at sitting on command, reward him intermittently.

Stay

Stay is the command used to keep a dog in one place. For example, it comes in handy when you're trying to keep your dog away from the door while you're bringing in groceries. Some trainers don't use this command at all, because they feel that the *sit* means "sit until you are told to get up," which is essentially the same thing as the *stay*. However, the *stay* command gives a dog the psychological cue that he will staying put for a longer time than in the *sit*. However, this command can be the most difficult thing to teach, especially if your Russell is still an energetic puppy. Every instinct that he has tells him to remain in motion, not stay still (unless, of course, he's asleep). If you can train him to stay for even 30 seconds, you should be proud of yourself. If you can get him to stay for a whole minute, both of you should get a treat!

How to Teach Stay

To teach this command, get a short lead and attach it to your dog. Give the *sit* command, and praise him. Then, with your palm held out in a "stop" gesture, back up slowly, saying "Stay." If your dog does indeed stay, praise him

FAMILY-FRIENDLY TIP

Children and Dog Training

Involve your child in dog training lessons, because doing so will help your Russell understand that the child is an authoritative figure who is able to request his obedience. Involving your child in the dog's training also provides a wonderful opportunity for you to teach her the importance of kind and consistent behavior around dogs. The degree of involvement depends on the age and maturity of your child, but some dog-savvy kids turn out to be better trainers than their parents!

and give him a treat. If he doesn't, say nothing, but quietly move him back to his original position and start again. Go only a very short distance—two or three steps—each time.

When your dog seems to understand the command, practice increasing the length of time that he stays, gradually working up to five minutes. When your Russell is able to remain in the stay for more than 30 seconds, try introducing a variable— moving around him while he remains sitting, for example. Then, slowly increase the distance between you, and walk in both directions. Next, try it outdoors in a fenced, secure area. Eventually, your dog should be able to stay for longer and longer periods. But please be patient.

Down

The *down* is an important command. A long down while you eat dinner, for example, will keep your dog's nose on the floor and not nudging against your plate. For some dogs, the *down* is a difficult skill. This is a position of great vulnerability, so a dominant dog will be slower to learn to *down* than will a more submissive one.

How to Teach Down

To lure your dog into the *down* position, hold a high-value treat near his nose and move your hand down between his forefeet. He should lie down to follow the treat. Say "Down," and praise him when he succeeds.

Tricks

Although dogs can get along perfectly well without ever having to learn a trick, teaching tricks is amusing for

you and fun for your dog. You can always amaze your friends, too.

Play Dead

Practice this trick when your dog has had his run of exercise, because you want him to be relaxed. Also, your dog should already know the *down* command for this trick.

To teach this trick, first tell your dog "Down." Most dogs seem to lean in one direction as they go down. When he is in position, gently push him over to one side and say "Play dead." Praise him and give him a gentle belly rub at the same time.

Training your Russell will help the two of you to bond.

Can an Old Dog Learn New Tricks?

Yes, older dogs can be taught new tricks. Simply use precisely the same techniques that you would with a puppy. Senior dogs, of course, should be given plenty of time to learn what you want. Some older dogs suffer from a condition called canine cognitive dysfunction, a type of canine senility. If you feel that your dog is confused and disoriented, talk to your vet. Medication is available.

Roll Over

Some dogs roll over naturally to greet you when you arrive home. If this is your dog, you can enhance the behavior by saying "Roll!" as he does it and rewarding him with a treat and praise. He will soon do it on command.

Shake Hands

Teaching your dog to shake hands is a wonderful way to bond with him and impress your family and friends. Any dog can learn this simple trick. Just hold a really tasty treat in your fist a few inches (cm) from your dog's chest. The dog may try to nibble at your fingers, a behavior that you should ignore, but eventually he'll start to paw at your hand. When he does, say "Shake!" and hand over the treat. Repeat this until he reliably shakes hands.

You can ratchet up a simple shake into a high-five by turning your palm so that it makes contact with your dog's paw in midair as he starts to shake. For still another variation, pull your hand back to encourage a "wave" from your dog.

Speak

Most dogs will bark at something, so to teach this trick correctly, find out what your dog's personal "bark signal" is. For example, if he barks when the doorbell sounds, ring the doorbell and say "Speak!" at the same time. Many dogs also bark if you hold up a piece of food and say "Want this, Spike? Want it? Speak!" and give him the treat when he does. Accompany or replace the auditory cue with a hand signal if you'd like. Soon, your dog will speak on command.

Your trained Russell may never land a role on a sitcom, but that's okay. You can enjoy him just as well at home. Besides, you never know when the agent might be calling—they're always looking for new talent!

Being Good

Chapter 7

In the

Doghouse

Before we get down to specifics, I would like to offer some general advice. A great number of problem behaviors in dogs occur simply because the animal does not get enough exercise. They say that a tired dog is a happy dog. Let me offer an amendment—a tired dog is a happy owner, and this is especially true with Russells.

Another way to prevent problem behaviors is by neutering your dog. Neutered dogs are less aggressive to dogs and to people, will be less inclined to mount, and will be less likely to wander. However, neutering will not make your Russell calmer or less destructive. If your dog is not yet neutered, get it done now. He will not only be healthier, but he will probably behave better, too. Only people who are actively engaged in showing dogs should have unneutered pets.

Finally, here's a third suggestion. Many problem behaviors have a medical cause, especially in cases where the dog has not visited the vet recently. If your dog suddenly starts behaving aggressively or "forgets" his housetraining, for example, take him to the vet for a thorough workup before assuming that the problem is psychologically based.

Barking

Barking is a normal component of canine behavior. Dogs bark to alert us to visitors, during play, and when they want something. Other dogs can read a lot into a dog's bark. They not only know that another dog is out there, but they can determine in what direction and how far away the dog is.

It is not possible or even desirable to eliminate all barking in our canine friends. However, sometimes

barking exceeds tolerable limits, and in these cases, the behavior must be dealt with. (Even if you don't mind it, you can bet the neighbors do.)

Excessive barking especially can be a serious problem in Russells. Unlike some other breeds, Russells are genetically programmed to bark and not just when they are bored or lonely. Some even seem to enjoy listening to

Barking is a normal component of canine behavior, but excessive barking must be controlled.

themselves bark, a behavior known as "recreational barking."

The Russell can also be an "alarm" barker, letting you know when you have visitors of any species. This isn't a bad thing—you want your dog to do his job. The problem begins when you can't shut the alarm off or when the dog barks for another reason, such as to guard his territory or to express his boredom and despair.

Solution

For the territorial barker, it may help to obscure the boundary beyond your house and your neighbor's by installing stockade-type fencing. Chain link allows the dog to see what's going on next door and causes him to pay far too much attention to it. If you hear him barking, bring him in immediately. That may be what he wants anyway, and who can blame him? Standing around all by oneself in the backyard isn't all that much fun. Most important, however, the barking may annoy the neighbors, and you don't want that.

If your Russell is barking because he's bored, the cure is simple: exercise! Healthy young Russells need more exercise than almost any other breed— at least two hours of it every day, and I don't mean a casual walk. You may

Finding a Behaviorist

If your dog's problem behavior is really serious, consult a dog behaviorist. This isn't always easy, though. As of this writing, there are only 38 board-certified veterinary behaviorists in the entire United States. However, certain trainers do specialize in particular problems. Your best bet is to ask your veterinarian to recommend a suitable trainer.

need to hire someone to play, jog, or swim with your dog, but the end result will be worth it. At the very least, try to give your dog a run before you go to work and after you come home.

If your Russell is barking due to a neurosis or separation anxiety, the cure lies in more training, work, play, and sensible, disciplined treatment. In serious cases, medication may be needed, at least temporarily. To minimize barking due to separation anxiety, keep the dog in a quiet part of your home, draw the blinds (darkness is calming), and leave the radio on, tuned to a talk station. This white noise masks other noises and comforts your dog with the sound of a human voice.

Begging

Begging can be so cute when it starts, especially when you look into those sad, imploring eyes. Before long, though, the cuteness has worn off and the behavior has become an irritation.

Why do dogs beg, anyway? Usually, their owners have taught them to do so by inadvertently reinforcing their begging with a reward, usually food. Dogs are so food oriented that giving in to them just once will turn a switch on in their little brains that is very hard to turn off.

Solution

If your Russell has already started to beg, you have two options to stop it. You can lock him in another part of the house while you eat. This is effective, although the dog may resort to barking—and it's not really a cure. Plus, it means that you'll have to separate him from the family every time you eat. However, if the dog is totally out of control (such as actually jumping on the table while you eat), it may be your only choice.

The second choice is really better, although it's more work. In this case, you simply do not reward the behavior. You completely

ignore it by not speaking to or looking at the dog. At first, the begging will increase as the dog tries harder and harder to get your attention. (If he gets out of hand, you can simply get up silently and remove him from the room for the rest of the meal, and then try again the next day). But do not give in, no matter what. If every family member and every guest goes along with the program, you can solve the problem.

Chewing

Most chewers are puppies who are trying to explore their world. However, if your energetic Russell is left alone without sufficient outlets for his

Redirect inappropriate chewing with an appropriate chew toy.

Parson & Jack Russell Terriers

restless mind and body, he can turn to destructive chewing. Other dogs may chew to relieve anxiety when they are left alone or exposed to loud noises.

Solution

The first step in treating the problem is to provide plenty of safe chewable items that are different enough from forbidden household items so that your puppy doesn't make a mistake. (You can't expect a dog to know an old shoe from a new one or a good t-shirt from a rag.) The second thing to do is to make sure that your dog gets enough exercise. You may have to wake up earlier, come home at noon, or hire a dog walker, but it's absolutely essential that your dog receive enough exercise. For short periods only, crating is an alternative. In some cases, drug therapy may be useful; consult your veterinarian for details.

Coprophagia

Coprophagia is a fancy name for stool eating. It's actually a rather normal behavior. Mother dogs eat their puppies' feces to keep that area clean, and young dogs tend to eat everything in their path, whether it's technically food or not. Most dogs eventually grow out of this unwholesome habit, but some do not. Some eat only their own feces, while others prefer the leavings of other dogs. Many can't resist cat feces, and few eat only frozen-solid feces they find around the yard in the

FAMILY-FRIENDLY TIP

Children and Dog Problem Behaviors

If a dog has a problem behavior, especially aggression, it is most likely to be directed at a child, because the dog probably correctly perceives her to be the weakest link in the family. This is why it's important never to allow a child to be alone with a dog who has shown aggressive behavior.

winter. No one knows exactly why dogs eat feces, although a number of theories have been advanced, including not enough mental and physical exercise and poor food.

Solution

Various home remedies have been suggested to solve the problem, but most of them really don't work very well. Your best strategy is to pick up your yard every day so that your Russell doesn't have the chance to indulge in this distasteful hobby. In some cases, a high-fiber diet has been shown to help, although no one really knows why. Giving your dog plenty of exercise is also beneficial—remember, a tired Russell is a well-behaved

86

Aggression

Aggression toward human beings can be very serious and is best handled by a professional. If your dog has ever bitten, snarled, or snapped at you, it's definitely time to call your vet. She will examine the dog to see if an underlying medical problem exists, and if there isn't, will be able to recommend a trainer who specializes in these cases.

Russell. In some few cases, anti-obsessional drugs have brought positive results, so talk to your vet if you want to explore this option.

Digging

Like all terriers, Russells are natural diggers. After all, the name "terrier" even means "earth dog." Although most terriers dig instinctively to find interesting prey (such as moles, gophers, and the like), some may also create craters to regulate their temperature. (A hole is cool in the summer and warm in the winter.) And, if your terrier digs near a fence, he may be trying to escape.

Solution

If your Russell is trying to escape, make sure that your fence extends under the ground a good bit to prevent him from digging an escape route underneath it. If he's just trying to find some shade, provide a shady place for his outdoor relaxation. If he's digging on instinct to find prey, though, you'll have to be more ingenious. One thing you can do is to make an "earthbox," which is like a sandbox full of soft dirt. Bury a bone or something similar (and let him see you do it) to motivate him, and he'll soon get the idea, hopefully leaving the rest of the yard alone. But don't count on it. Dogs can hear moles and mice underground, so you may have to supervise him while outdoors if the holes bother you.

Jumping Up

You know the routine. You come home or a beloved guest arrives, and the next thing you know, your Russell is leaping ecstatically in the air, more often than not making unwelcome contact with you or your guest's face and head. But don't blame your Russell. Many dogs jump because we have taught them to jump. In fact, if your Russell never received encouragement for doing this as a puppy, he wouldn't be doing it now. Fortunately, it's never too late to make a change, although it does require an unwavering consistency on the part of you and your guests to make it work.

Solution

The best way to get your dog to stop jumping is not to reward that behavior—not with a look, not with a sound, and certainly not with a kick or knee in his chest. When your dog jumps, simply fold your arms and look away. Do not respond. If he continues, walk away and don't look at him. When he ceases to jump, immediately get down to his level and reward him with praise and attention. After a week or so, he will get the idea. The key is to make sure that everyone understands and commits to the technique—consistency is crucial to solving this problem behavior.

Noise Phobias

Fear of loud noises is common in dogs and for a reason—loud noises are threatening. A phobia, however, goes beyond ordinary fear; it is excessive, persistent, and irrational. You can tell if your dog is phobic if he becomes rigid, paces, trembles, pants, shakes, salivates, hides, or whines at the fear-eliciting sound.

Both fears and phobias can develop at any age in a dog. Some arise after one frightening episode; others develop over time. If the fearful stimulus occurs frequently, the fears are enforced, and the phobia increases. In general, dogs do not "get over" a phobia. In fact, what may start as a simple phobia over one noise, like thunder, may generalize to fear over any loud noise.

Solution

To alleviate your dog's phobia, it is important not exacerbate his fear by

Like all terriers, Russells are natural diggers.

When dealing with separation anxiety, avoid long, emotion-laden goodbyes.

or bite themselves excessively. You will see hair loss, sores, or rashes on the affected part of the body. The causes may be medical or psychological.

Solution

If the cause is medical, the self-mutilating behavior usually resolves once the underlying condition is treated, although the behavior may remain even after the medical problem has been addressed. For example, the problem may begin as a simple flea bite or infection but progress to an obsession in which the dog cannot leave his foot alone. This is considered an obsessive-compulsive disorder. Other psychological factors that may lead to self-mutilation include anxiety, stress caused by long periods of confinement, isolation, harassment from another pet, or repeated exposure to scary noises.

In earlier stages of this disorder, you can try to distract or redirect the behavior. Try getting your dog to play with you or to chew on a chew toy. However, in many cases, once the behavior settles in, you really need to seek professional help.

Your vet will perform a physical examination and perhaps take a skin scraping or do an allergy test; he may ask for a blood test or chemistry profile. If medical causes are ruled out, he will recommend that you do your best to remove the stressors in your

either punishing or attempting to soothe him. Just ignore it, and act happy and cheerful. Although some people have had success using counter-conditioning and other training techniques, noise phobias usually respond best to drug therapy. Talk to your vet.

Self-Mutilation

Self-mutilation occurs when dogs lick

keep any ownership records you have—registration or adoption paperwork, vet bills, and so on. None of these will prove to the authorities that the dog on the paperwork is the dog that you are looking for, but they help. Your best bet may be a clear picture of you and your dog together in happier times.

If you do lose your dog, make up flyers immediately (don't wait even an hour) and place them on every legal place that you can find. The flyer should contain the dog's photo and description and your phone number in big letters.

Go door to door in your neighborhood and talk to everyone. (Don't go by yourself unless you really know your neighbors.) Give everyone a flyer. Offer a reward—as much as you can afford. That will motivate kids to help look, and they are creative lookers!

Check with every vet, animal shelter, and rescue organization in the area. Keep checking. Go there personally and repeatedly, and take a look at the captive dogs yourself. (Some shelter volunteers can't tell a Russell from a Rottweiler.) Put ads in the newspaper that offer a reward.

If your dog has been injured, he may hide in places that you wouldn't ordinarily think of. Friendly dogs will most likely seek out human beings; shy dogs or loners are more likely to be found in more isolated places. An old hunting trick is to put out some unwashed clothes that carry your scent. This is especially useful if your dog has disappeared in a place with which he is not familiar. Check the area frequently.

If you are lucky enough to find your precious lost dog, don't forget to pick up the flyers that you posted around town. Also, please let people who helped you know that your pet has been found at last.

Sometimes dogs run away, not because you are abusing them, but because they are curious about what lies beyond the backyard. If this happens to you and your dog, you must maximize his chances of a safe return.

The easiest step in finding a lost dog is also the most important. Put an ID tag on that collar, and make sure that the information stays current. This is your best chance of getting your dog back. The ID tag should have your name, telephone number (including area code), and address. Check it every day to make sure that it is still present and legible. Also, get a license, and put it on the collar. (This is probably the law in your area anyway.) Always keep recent photos (both color and black and white) of your dog in your files.

If you have a website, include a series of photos showing different views; your lost dog posters can direct people to your website. You may also need to prove that the dog is yours, so

SENIOR DOG TIP

Seniors Dogs and Problem Behaviors

Although senior dogs present far fewer problem behaviors than puppies do, you can expect some behavioral changes related to aging. The most common is a loss of housetraining and a certain grumpiness of temperament. Both of these are usually medically rather than psychologically based.

On the whole, you will find your older dog to be a behavioral delight. He won't shred the carpet, rip up your dissertation, or chase after cars. Older dogs are generally polite and calm pets—and excellent prospects for adoption. Many come already trained. If you don't want to go through the chewing-peeing-ripping stage, consider adopting a senior Russell Terrier.

dog's life. In some cases, he may prescribe anti-obsessional medication.

Separation Anxiety

Some Russells suffer from separation anxiety when left alone for long periods. Separation anxiety is common because dogs are pack animals who do not enjoy being left alone. (Remember, we have created dogs to be dependent on us, so we shouldn't be surprised when they are!)

Dogs who suffer from separation anxiety bark, cry, chew themselves or furniture, urinate, and scratch doors to pieces. Owners can actually inadvertently reinforce this behavior when they return at the first cry and try to comfort the animal.

Solution

To deal with the behavior, avoid long, emotion-laden goodbyes and exuberant greetings. Be calm and matter-of-fact. Totally ignore your dog for the first few minutes after you come home. (This is tough, but it works.) Practice taking very short absences (just a minute or two) and very gradually increase them. If these techniques don't seem to be working, consult your vet, who can recommend a professional behaviorist and/or medication to treat the problem.

Submissive Urination

Submissive urination is a common condition of young puppies and shy dogs who urinate when reprimanded. Most dogs outgrow this behavior as long as you do nothing to encourage it.

Solution

The only correct response to submissive urination is not to respond to the behavior. Just walk away and

clean it up after a few minutes. (If you clean it up immediately, some dogs get the idea that what they have done is intriguing to you, and they may try to repeat it.) Because this behavior usually occurs when greeting, try saying hello to your dog in a less threatening way. For example, try kneeling down and averting your eyes from his face. Also, pet him under the chest rather than on the head.

If your dog engages in inappropriate urination only when you are looking at him, it is almost surely submissive urination. However, loss of housetraining at other times could signal a medical condition, such as a urinary tract infection. Talk to your vet if you suspect that this is the case.

It is impossible to bring up a dog without running into a few snags in the road. Just like children, dogs are complex creatures who can exhibit a variety of problem behaviors. If you're smarter than your Russell, you can learn to prevent or solve any problems that may occur.

Chapter 8

Stepping Out

The Russell Terrier is the anti-couch potato. This energetic dog thrives on physical activity and likes it best when you join him. Luckily, you and your best buddy can participate together in multitudes of enjoyable activities. Put down the coffee cup, turn off the television, and start exploring them!

Travel

What is a vacation without your faithful Russell as your side? Nothing at all, that's what!

To prepare for the fateful event, you need to take care of just a few little things. First, make sure that your dog is healthy enough to travel. Get him checked out within two weeks of the big day. The last thing you need is to have a sick dog on your hands while you're trying to ski the slopes or lounge on the beach. Make sure that he's up-to-date on vaccines. Get a copy of all his records while you are at your vet, and take them with you, especially if you are crossing state lines. Be sure to bring any medications he's taking as well.

I know that your Russell always wears his collar and ID tags, but they are especially important when you're traveling. Double-check that you have them! Also, be sure to bring enough food, toys, water, and bedding—and don't forget his crate or carrier.

By Car

Your Russell's car trip should begin before yours does. Most dogs love to ride in the car, but the excitement of the trip can have unfortunate consequences, such as whining or even vomiting and diarrhea—not from carsickness but from the sheer thrill of it all. One way to cut down on the chance of all this is to exercise your dog to tire him out or at least calm him down before you hit the road.

Keep your car at a cool and comfortable temperature for your pet. Dogs tend to become very excited and anxious in the car, and what seems comfy for you may be unbearably hot for him. Open the window a crack, and get some nice fresh air in there.

Never leave your dog unattended in the car. It may be a pleasant 80°F (26.7°C) outside, but the temperature inside your vehicle can hit a lethal 140°F (60°C)

Bring Your Own Water

Dogs, especially when excited, pant and drool a lot and can quickly become dehydrated. To reduce the chances of dehydration, bring along a canteen with a plastic dish attached. Many companies make special traveling water and food containers, some of which are soft-sided for easy handling and storage. Bringing your own water is especially important for puppies. Young animals are very sensitive to water changes and can acquire a bad case of diarrhea from drinking strange water. And believe me, puppy diarrhea is the last thing you want to deal with while on vacation.

really quickly. Puppies are especially vulnerable to heat stress. A good rule is to never leave your dog in a closed car if the temperature outside is more than 55°F (12.8°C) in the shade. If you absolutely must leave your dog in the car for a few minutes, do as many of the following as possible:

• Park in the shade.
• Leave your car running with the air conditioning on and your dog in a crate. Get extra keys if you lock the doors.
• Open the windows as wide as you feel that you safely can.
• Put a cold wet towel over the crate.
• Check your pet often.
• Leave a note on the windshield stating where you are in case of an emergency.
• Make sure that your dog has access to fresh water.

Seat Belts

As a rule, your dog should ride safely in the back seat with a proper doggy seatbelt, or he should be confined to the crate. Both methods safely restrain your dog, keeping both you and him safe. Having a Russell leap into your lap while you're trying to negotiate a difficult turn can be dangerous, and unanticipated sharp stops could hurl your Russell into the windshield.

Pickup Trucks

Do not allow your dog to ride in the

The energetic Russell Terrier thrives on physical activity and likes it best when you join him.

back of a pickup truck. This is unkind and dangerous. Dogs can jump out of trucks or be thrown out and be severely hurt or killed. Even the special dog harnesses used to keep them from bouncing out of a truck do nothing to protect your Russell's eyes from flying debris. If he must ride in the back of a truck, place him in a heavy-duty plastic crate that protects his eyes from dirt

Packing for Your Dog

If you are going to be gone for any length of time, pack a little suitcase for your Russell that includes water bowls, bedding, flea and tick prevention, extra ID, grooming tools, paper towels, leashes, toys, health records, and medicine.

and pebbles. You can secure the dog's crate in the cargo area.

Carsickness

One good way to avoid carsickness is to begin travel training early—between seven and nine weeks of age is ideal. This is simply nothing more than taking your dog out for gradually lengthening trips.

If your dog has a tendency toward carsickness, it's usually best not to feed him four to six hours before the trip. (Even if he does throw up, it won't be quite so bad.) Remember to keep the car cool, and bring paper towels with you, just in case.

Some dogs do not get carsick if kept in a well-ventilated crate that discourages them from looking backward. Uncrated in the back seat, some dogs start gazing out the back window, which can make them woozy. Even most Russells aren't smart enough to know that if they just turned around, they'd feel better.

To further help prevent carsickness, stop frequently when traveling to give your dog a breather and a bit of

Allowing your Russell Terrier to ride loose in the car is dangerous both for him and for the driver.

exercise. Also, when parking, turn off the motor. Gas fumes from the engine can make pets and people sick.

Often, your pet may become sick in the car for psychological reasons. He may know that you only take him to "negative" places, like the vet— exactly where he doesn't want to go. Make trips a joy for him by taking him to fun places, and see if his carsickness improves.

Certain medications can help stop canine carsickness, so consult your veterinarian for more information. Some people also use holistic remedies for carsickness. Chief among these is ginger, which can be bought in capsules or as an extract at a health food store. Ask a qualified animal herbalist or your vet for the proper dosage. If you don't happen to know a qualified animal herbalist or don't have time to query the vet, a ginger snap cookie or two will be fine.

By Air

Many airlines and state health officials require health certificates issued by a licensed veterinarian within ten days of the scheduled flight, so have your Russell checked out within that time. The United States Department of Agriculture produces an excellent booklet detailing federal regulations called "Traveling by Air With Your Pet," and you can get it by calling 301-734-7833. The ASPCA also has a pamphlet with the same basic information. Rules

FAMILY-FRIENDLY TIP

Traveling With Kids and Dogs

If you are traveling with your dog and your child, you really have your work cut out for you! In this case, it is absolutely critical that the dog be safely crated. A heedless child could easily fling open the car door upon arrival, only to have the dog leap out of the car and be gone forever.

change frequently, so always check with the airline before you go. In addition, the same rules do not necessarily apply to all of them. Generally, dogs must be at least eight weeks old and weaned at the time of flight. Airlines will not transport pets in temperatures below 32°F (0°C) or above 85°F (29.4°C). So if you're traveling in the summer, plan the trip for the morning, and if you're traveling in the winter, plan the trip for the afternoon.

If possible, schedule a direct, nonstop flight. It's less stressful for your pet and will reduce his chances of being lost. (This can indeed happen; some airlines treat pets more like luggage than passengers!) Try to schedule flights during less busy times, too.

Crate your dog in an approved container, and attach all necessary instructions to it. Approved containers allow the dog to sit, lie down, stand, and turn around. The floor of the container must be solid and covered with absorbent lining or litter. Pegboard flooring is not allowed. The words "Live Animal" must be written clearly on the crate. Include arrows or the words "This End Up" to make sure that your pet doesn't get transported upside down. You should also print directions reading "Keep Away From Hot Sun and Extreme Cold" and hope that somebody pays attention. Secure the crate firmly, but do not lock it. It's more likely that someone will need to reach your pet to help him than it is likely that someone will steal him.

Kennels must be ventilated, and the rules are quite specific about it. At least 14 percent of the total wall space must be ventilated, with at least one-third of the opening located in the top half of the kennel. (You don't actually have to calculate the percentages. Most commercial crates state whether or not they are airline approved.) Remember to put a favorite toy or an old sock of yours in the kennel. Things with your scent will keep your Russell comfortable and happy.

Your pet needs a flat, buckle collar with two identification tags firmly attached. Never use a choke chain. Of course, you'll include your name and a phone number where you can actually be reached during your pet's flight time. Also, provide food, water, and any necessary medical information. If your dog needs medication, attach it to the side of the crate in case of emergency, along with complete directions about its use. Food and water dishes must be securely attached to the sides of the crate.

Airlines are not required to carry pets at all and may refuse to do so for any reason whatsoever. Rules can also change overnight. This is why it's important to do your research in advance to avoid any unpleasant surprises once you get to the airport.

SENIOR DOG TIP

Traveling With an Older Dog

Older dogs can be transported safely if you take extra care to keep them comfortable. They don't have the ability to regulate their temperature as well as young dogs do, and so they need to be kept warm in cool weather and cool in warm weather. Older dogs get stiff, too, and so need frequent stops to loosen their joints.

Accommodations

According to a survey taken by the American Animal Hospital Association (AAHA), 41 percent of pet owners take their pets along on vacations, at least sometimes. Some hotels allow pets, but you need to inquire first. Expect to put down a deposit or even an extra fee, because hotels look poorly upon having their carpets and furniture eaten or urinated on.

Most motels will not allow you to leave your pet alone in the room. Some require that he be kept crated at all times, even when you are there. This is another excellent reason to crate train your pet. If you must go out, leave the dog inside and put a "Do Not Disturb" sign on the door so that the maid won't decide to wander in, make the bed, and play with your Russell while you're gone.

It's disturbing, but the number of motels and hotels who do accept dogs has dropped by 25 percent in recent years. It's very important for dogs and their owners everywhere to make a good impression on hotel management and staff. People make decisions about welcoming dogs based on the behavior of those who have gone before. If your dog is not well behaved in every way, then leave him at home.

A well-trained Russell Terrier may be a good candidate for the Canine Good Citizen test.

Stepping Out

Canine Good Citizen

One of the best ways to prepare your Russell for all sorts of activities is to help him earn his Canine Good Citizen (CGC) certificate. This ten-step test is open to all dogs and will help prepare your Russell for more advanced obedience and sporting work.

The only equipment you need is a leash, buckle or slip collar, and a brush or comb. A 20-foot (6.1 m) lead will be supplied by the evaluator. Your dog must pass all the following tests to get the certificate:

- *Test 1:* Accepting a friendly stranger
- *Test 2:* Sitting politely for petting
- *Test 3:* Appearance and grooming

- *Test 4:* Out for a walk (walking on a loose lead)
- *Test 5:* Walking through a crowd
- *Test 6:* Sit and down on command and staying in place
- *Test 7:* Coming when called
- *Test 8:* Reaction to another dog
- *Test 9:* Reaction to distraction
- *Test 10:* Supervised separation

Therapy Work

Some of the most rewarding activities you can participate in are animal-assisted activities (AAA) or animal-assisted therapy (AAT). Although these terms sound pretty similar, there are some differences between them.

Animal-assisted activities are mostly the casual "meet and greet" activities that involve pets visiting people in hospitals, prisons, and nursing homes. In these cases, the primary job of the animal is to relieve loneliness and stress, not to provide specific therapy for specific patients or for a specified medical condition. You won't have to take notes, and in general, you can stay as long as you and the client wish.

Animal-assisted therapy, on the other hand, is specifically designed to promote improvement in human physical, social, emotional, or thinking skills.

This process is more formal and requires more training on the part of the handler and dog.

Participating in animal-assisted activities or therapy is a wonderful opportunity for you and your well-socialized, well-groomed dog to bring happiness to people who really need it. For more information, look online or call a local hospital or nursing home to see what programs are available.

Sports

If your interests lie more in highly active competitive activities, you have plenty from which to choose—but choose carefully. Some sports are open

In the sport of agility, a dog must navigate a timed obstacle course.

to all dogs, and some are open only to purebreds. Some are only available to AKC-registered Parson Russell Terriers, and some are only available to JRTCA-registered Jack Russell Terriers. Always check with the sponsoring group to see if your dog will be able to join in.

Agility

In this event, a dog navigates a maze of obstacles, including tires, tunnels, an A-frame, a dogwalk, and a teeter-totter. No set rule exists about a course layout; each one is different. The judge determines a standard course time (SCT) that sets the parameters for the completion of the course. Handlers are permitted any number of verbal or hand signals to help their dogs navigate the obstacles, but they are not allowed to touch them.

Conformation (Showing)

Conformation shows (dog shows) are beauty contests for dogs. The JRTCA and AKC both hold such events, with the winner in each case the dog who most closely meets the breed standard, which is slightly different for each organization. The dogs are judged on conformation (looks), movement, and temperament. Winning dogs not only look good, but they are impeccably groomed, sociable, and well behaved on a leash.

Showing dogs sounds simple, but there is more to handling a show dog than meets the eye. To have the best chance of winning, sign up for a handling class at your nearest kennel club.

Earth Events

In earth events, which simulate real hunting situations, the dog enters a tunnel and attempts to find a quarry (a rat in a cage) at the end of the tunnel. The tunnel has several turns to make it more difficult. The dog with the fastest time to the quarry is considered the winner. The terrier must mark (i.e., bark, scratch, whine) to qualify the time. This event has various divisions, including novice, open puppy, open adult, and junior handler (optional).

Both the AKC and JRTCA hold these digging contests, which are called "go-to-ground" in JRTCA parlance and "earth trials" in AKC language.

Flyball

Flyball is a relatively new sport at which Russell Terriers really excel. It's a race in which dogs leap over a series of jumps, run to a box, grab a ball, and race back to the start line. This relay race is controlled by its own association, the North American Flyball Association (NAFA), and is not part of official AKC or JRTCA activities.

Obedience

In this event, the dog and handler are required to perform a series of exercises that test the obedience of the terrier. Exercises may include (depending on the level), heeling, the sit and long down, scent discrimination, directed jumping, and other events. Each exercise is graded by the obedience judge. Points may be subtracted for minor and substantial faults. Divisions include Sub-Novice, Novice, Open, Utility, Brace, and Junior Handler.

Both the JRTCA and AKC hold obedience trials, although rules vary slightly.

Racing

In this exciting event, the dogs race down a straight course with a starting box at one end and a stack of straw bales at the other. Some courses are flat; others have hurdles. The dogs chase a lure, usually a piece of scented fur, that is attached to a string operated by a generator. The winner is the first dog who gets through the holes in the bales and crosses the finish line. Dogs are muzzled for safety.

This sport is recognized by the JRTCA only.

Trailing and Locating, and Tracking

Trailing and locating is a JRTCA event that involves the terrier tracking and locating a "quarry" above ground. Because no real quarry exists, at least usually, an imaginary one is created from a scent mixture of fox urine, water, and unscented glycerin. The terrier is judged on his ability to follow the trail in a simulated natural hunting environment to locate, mark, and chase after the quarry. The terrier is judged

The Expert Knows

Safety First

No matter what activity you decide to explore with your dog, think safety. Have your terrier checked out by the vet before you begin, train sensibly, and find a mentor to help you in your chosen sport. Also, avoid competing when it is very hot or bitterly cold.

on a combination of time and accuracy, so the animal with the fastest time is not necessarily the winner. Various classes are offered.

The AKC offers a class in tracking, which is open to all breeds, in which the dog follows a human scent usually placed on a leather glove. Russell Terriers are usually more interested in following fox trails, though. That's what they were bred for!

Games and Activities

Not everyone has a taste for competition; some people simply prefer spending time with their dogs. If this is you, grab your leash and head for the hills. (If truth be told, most dogs prefer a rigorous woodland hike than all the dog shows in the world anyway.)

Hiking

Hiking is fun, free, and fabulous. In fact, nothing beats a vigorous hike in the woods with your Russell. You'll feel better, lose weight, and bond with your dog. Just remember to bring enough water for your pal, and keep him on a leash, because Russells are very likely to take off chasing anything that

moves, leaving you standing there with your mouth hanging open.

If it's very hot or cold, make your hikes short. In the heat, take walks in the early morning or late afternoon. If you go out at night, be sure to use reflectors on your dog's collar as well as on your own clothes. Very rocky paths are not comfortable for your Russell, so stick to grass or dirt paths as much as possible.

Retrieving

Some dogs are natural retrievers. Others are "half retrievers." In other words, they will run after the ball but refuse to bring it back. In fact, they often run in the opposite direction, changing the game from "fetch" to "tag." To help your dog play by your rules, try this. As soon as you see him grab the thrown toy, instead of standing around waiting for him to bring it to you, run in the opposite direction. Most dogs will immediately try to catch up with you. When he does, take the toy, praise him lavishly, and give him a treat. Soon you won't have to run away; he'll be glad to bring the toy back for a treat.

Your Russell Terrier longs to be an active part of your life. Make it happen! You'll both be happier and healthier.

Resources

Associations and Organizations

Breed Clubs

American Kennel Club (AKC)
5580 Centerview Drive
Raleigh, NC 27606
Telephone: (919) 233-9767
Fax: (919) 233-3627
E-mail: info@akc.org
www.akc.org

Canadian Kennel Club (CKC)
89 Skyway Avenue, Suite 100
Etobicoke, Ontario M9W 6R4
Telephone: (416) 675-5511
Fax: (416) 675-6506
E-mail: information@ckc.ca
www.ckc.ca

Federation Cynologique Internationale (FCI)
Secretariat General de la FCI
Place Albert 1er, 13
B – 6530 Thuin
Belqique
www.fci.be

Jack Russell Terrier Club of America (JRTCA)
P.O. Box 4527
Lutherville, MD 21094-4527
Telephone: (410) 561-3655
Fax: (410) 560-2563
E-mail: JRTCA@worldnet.att.net
www.jrtca.com

The Kennel Club
1 Clarges Street
London
W1J 8AB
Telephone: 0870 606 6750
Fax: 0207 518 1058
www.the-kennel-club.org.uk

United Kennel Club (UKC)
100 E. Kilgore Road
Kalamazoo, MI 49002-5584
Telephone: (269) 343-9020
Fax: (269) 343-7037
E-mail: pbickell@ukcdogs.com
www.ukcdogs.com

Pet Sitters

National Association of Professional Pet Sitters
15000 Commerce Parkway, Suite C
Mt. Laurel, New Jersey 08054
Telephone: (856) 439-0324
Fax: (856) 439-0525
E-mail: napps@ahint.com
www.petsitters.org

Pet Sitters International
201 East King Street
King, NC 27021-9161
Telephone: (336) 983-9222
Fax: (336) 983-5266
E-mail: info@petsit.com
www.petsit.com

Rescue Organizations and Animal Welfare Groups

American Humane Association (AHA)
63 Inverness Drive East
Englewood, CO 80112
Telephone: (303) 792-9900
Fax: 792-5333
www.americanhumane.org

American Society for the Prevention of Cruelty to Animals (ASPCA)
424 E. 92nd Street
New York, NY 10128-6804
Telephone: (212) 876-7700
www.aspca.org

Royal Society for the Prevention of Cruelty to Animals (RSPCA)
Telephone: 0870 3335 999
Fax: 0870 7530 284
www.rspca.org.uk

The Humane Society of the United States (HSUS)
2100 L Street, NW
Washington DC 20037
Telephone: (202) 452-1100
www.hsus.org

Sports

Canine Freestyle Federation, Inc.
Secretary: Brandy Clymire
E-Mail: secretary@canine-freestyle.org
www.canine-freestyle.org

International Agility Link (IAL)
Global Administrator: Steve Drinkwater
E-mail: yunde@powerup.au
www.agilityclick.com/~ial

North American Dog Agility Council
11522 South Hwy 3
Cataldo, ID 83810
www.nadac.com

North American Flyball Association
www.flyball.org
1400 West Devon Avenue #512
Chicago, IL 6066
800-318-6312

United States Dog Agility Association
P.O. Box 850955
Richardson, TX 75085-0955
Telephone: (972) 487-2200
www.usdaa.com

World Canine Freestyle Organization
P.O. Box 350122
Brooklyn, NY 11235-2525
Telephone: (718) 332-8336
www.worldcaninefreestyle.org

Therapy

Delta Society
875 124th Ave NE, Suite 101
Bellevue, WA 98005
Telephone: (425) 226-7357
Fax: (425) 235-1076
E-mail: info@deltasociety.org
www.deltasociety.org

Therapy Dogs Incorporated
PO Box 5868
Cheyenne, WY 82003
Telephone: (877) 843-7364
E-mail: therdog@sisna.com
www.therapydogs.com

Therapy Dogs International (TDI)
88 Bartley Road
Flanders, NJ 07836
Telephone: (973) 252-9800
Fax: (973) 252-7171
E-mail: tdi@gti.net
www.tdi-dog.org

Training
Association of Pet Dog Trainers (APDT)
150 Executive Center Drive Box 35
Greenville, SC 29615
Telephone: (800) PET-DOGS
Fax: (864) 331-0767
E-mail: information@apdt.com
www.apdt.com

National Association of Dog Obedience Instructors (NADOI)
PMB 369
729 Grapevine Hwy.
Hurst, TX 76054-2085
www.nadoi.org

Veterinary and Health Resources
American Animal Hospital Association (AAHA)
P.O. Box 150899
Denver, CO 80215-0899
Telephone: (303) 986-2800
Fax: (303) 986-1700
E-mail: info@aahanet.org
www.aahanet.org/index.cfm

American Holistic Veterinary Medical Association (AHVMA)
2218 Old Emmorton Road
Bel Air, MD 21015
Telephone: (410) 569-0795
Fax: (410) 569-2346
E-mail: office@ahvma.org
www.ahvma.org

American Veterinary Medical Association (AVMA)
1931 North Meacham Road – Suite 100
Schaumburg, IL 60173
Telephone: (847) 925-8070
Fax: (847) 925-1329
E-mail: avmainfo@avma.org
www.avma.org

ASPCA Animal Poison Control Center
1717 South Philo Road, Suite 36
Urbana, IL 61802
Telephone: (888) 426-4435
www.aspca.org

British Veterinary Association (BVA)
7 Mansfield Street
London
W1G 9NQ
Telephone: 020 7636 6541
Fax: 020 7436 2970
E-mail: bvahq@bva.co.uk
www.bva.co.uk

Canine Eye Registration Foundation (CERF)
VMDB/CERF
1248 Lynn Hall
625 Harrison St.
Purdue University
West Lafayette, IN 47907-2026
Telephone: (765) 494-8179
E-mail: CERF@vmbd.org
www.vmdb.org

Publications

Books

Anderson, Teoti. *The Super Simple Guide to Housetraining*. Neptune City: TFH Publications, 2004.

Boneham, Sheila, Ph.D. *The Parson & Jack Russell Terriers*. Neptune City: TFH Publications, 2006.

Morgan, Diane. *Good Dogkeeping*. Neptune City: TFH Publications, 2005.

Magazines

AKC *Family Dog*
American Kennel Club
260 Madison Avenue
New York, NY 10016
Telephone: (800) 490-5675
E-mail: familydog@akc.org
www.akc.org/pubs/familydog

Dog & Kennel
Pet Publishing, Inc.
7-L Dundas Circle
Greensboro, NC 27407
Telephone: (336) 292-4272
Fax: (336) 292-4272
E-mail: info@petpublishing.com
www.dogandkennel.com

Dog Fancy
Subscription Department
P.O. Box 53264
Boulder, CO 80322-3264
Telephone: (800) 365-4421
E-mail: barkback@dogfancy.com
www.dogfancy.com

Dogs Monthly
Ascot House
High Street, Ascot,
Berkshire SL5 7JG
United Kingdom
Telephone: 0870 730 8433
Fax: 0870 730 8431
E-mail: admin@rtc-associates.freeserve.co.uk
www.corsini.co.uk/dogsmonthly

Index

Note: Boldface numbers indicate illustrations.

108

Parson & Jack Russell Terriers

Index

Dedication

To the Reverend John Russell, who made it all possible, and to John Hepfer, whose heroic efforts have saved many canine lives.

Acknowledgments

Thanks to Stephanie Fornino for her superb editing, support, and laughter.

About the Author

In her spare time (away from her animals), Diane Morgan is an assistant professor of philosophy and religion at Wilson College, Chambersburg, PA. She has authored numerous books on canine care and nutrition and has also written many breed books, horse books, and books on Eastern philosophy and religion. She is an avid gardener (and writes about that, too). Diane lives in Williamsport, Maryland with several dogs, two cats, some fish, and a couple of humans.

Photo Credits

Front cover photo courtesy of Stephen Walls (Shutterstock).
Photo on page 36 courtesy of Paulette Braun.
Photo on page 7 courtesy of Tara Darling.
Photo on page 68 courtesy of Judith E. Strom.
Photo on page 14 courtesy of Lynn Watson (Shutterstock).
Photo on page 99 courtesy of Alison Woollard (Shutterstock).
Photo on page 65 courtesy of Jeffrey Ong Guo Xiong (Shutterstock).

REACH OUT. ACT. RESPOND.
Go to AnimalPlanet.com/ROAR and find out how you can be a voice for animals everywhere!